ON THE
EMMAUS
ROAD

A Guide for Transitions in Ordained Leadership

MARY BRENNAN THORPE

CHURCH
PUBLISHING
INCORPORATED

Church Publishing
19 East 34th Street
New York, NY 10016
www.churchpublishing.org

Cover icon by Mary Brennan Thorpe
Cover design by Marc Whitaker, MTWdesign
Typeset by Rose Design

A record of this book is available from the Library of Congress.

ISBN-13: 978-1-64065-301-6 (paperback)
ISBN-13: 978-1-64065-302-3 (ebook)

In gratitude for the bishops, colleagues, lay leaders, parishes,
and friends who informed and encouraged this work,
because your gifts and graces shine throughout this book.

No words are enough for Doug, my encourager and partner
in life, love, and writing. I am blessed.

CONTENTS

Preface vii

I. Introduction 1
The Structure of This Book   1

II. A General Outline of the Transition Process 3

III. For the Departing Priest 8

IV. For the Vestry: Phase One 13

    a. Vestry Involvement in the Process: A Quick View
      from 10,000 Feet   13

    b. Planning a "Good Goodbye"   17

    c. Options for Calls: A Closer Look   18

    d. Securing an Interim   20

    e. Calling a Priest-in-Charge Rather Than Using
      an Interim Rector   22

    f. Selecting a Discernment Committee
      and Committee Chair   24

    g. What Is the Work of the Discernment Committee?   27

    h. The Commissioning of a Discernment Committee   28

V. Other Vestry Considerations 30

    a. Communications during the Time of Transition   30

    b. Staff Issues   32

VI. Particular Considerations for Challenged Parishes
and for Challenging Times 34

    a. Challenged Parishes: Growing Smaller and Poorer   34

    b. Challenged Parishes: Bad/Sad/Mad Endings   38

    c. Challenging Times   41

VII. For the Discernment Committee: Phase One 45

    a. An Overview of the Work Ahead   46

    b. Communications and Vestry/Committee Interactions
      during the Time of Transition   49

    c. The Self-Study Process 51

    d. Tools for Self-Study 51

    e. Mind the Gap: Bridging Information-Gathering
       between "Who Are We Now" and "Who Is God
       Calling Us to Be Next?" 68

    f. Preparing the Community Ministry Portfolio 72

    g. It's Done! 74

    h. Promoting Your Position 75

 VIII. For the Vestry: Phase Two 77

   IX. For the Discernment Committee: Phase Two
      and Final Steps 80

    a. The Spiritual Nature of the Work You Do 81

    b. First Stage Interviewing 84

    c. Behavioral Interview Guide 86

    d. Short-List Work 89

    e. On the Road: Visiting Candidates in Their Own Parish 90

    f. For the Discernment Committee: Final Phase 94

   X. For the Vestry: Final Steps 96

    a. One More Goodbye: To Your Interim Rector 98

    b. Welcoming Your New Priest 98

    c. When Something Goes Sideways 104

    d. How the Diocese Welcomes Your New Priest 105

   XI. Last Words 106

Appendix A: Sample Surveys 107

Appendix B: Some Guidelines for the Conduct of Focus Groups . . . 129

Appendix C: Appreciative Inquiry-Style Congregational Meeting . . . 133

Appendix D: Community Ministry Profile Worksheet. 137

PREFACE

Eighty-four calls.

Since I began this work of transition ministry several years ago, we've midwifed more than one hundred calls for rectors, vicars, priests-in-charge, and deacons-in-charge in this diocese. Add in the facilitation of appointments of a number of interim rectors, and it's safe to say that almost every possible mistake has been made, a great number of unusual situations have been faced, a range of all possible emotions felt.

So consider this book, based upon research as well as the lived experience of transition in Episcopal churches of incredible variety, your way to avoid repeating mistakes you don't need to make, a way to navigate the usual pitfalls, a way to see the goal clearly and move toward it confidently.

What's the goal?

Here's what it is not: hiring a priest. You're not contracting with a plumber (although many of us have plunged a few toilets in our parishes). You're not figuring out who the best heart surgeon is to fix your ticker (although many of us have sat with and wept with and prayed with parishioners with broken hearts). You're not hiring a lawyer to sort out who owes who what when someone has cheated you (although many of us have facilitated knotty and painful conversations between those whose relationships have been torn).

You're seeking God's will for your parish in the next chapter of its story, and discerning what spiritual leader will help you write that chapter.

That might seem a bit intimidating—how do we hear God's voice?—but this book will help you get there. Through process, prayer, wisdom from those who have done this before, you will find the priest you need, and you might find that as the process evolves, this experience will be spiritually transformative.

The title?

The metaphor of journey is often used to describe the call of a new ordained leader, and sometimes jokingly people say that they felt like the

Israelites in the wilderness, searching for the Promised Land over a forty-year span. That's a dark image, and a frightening one.

So perhaps another journey metaphor is more helpful, and more apt. Consider the two disciples walking to Emmaus after the resurrection (Luke 24:13–35). Cleopas and a companion are walking home. Jesus has risen from the dead, but they don't understand that yet. They're talking about everything that had happened, perhaps feeling a little traumatized by it all. They encounter a stranger. They share this weird story, and how disappointed they were that things didn't turn out the way they'd hoped. The stranger instructs them to think about it differently. They still are distracted and can't wrap their minds around it. It is only later that evening, when they eat dinner together, when the stranger breaks the bread and blesses it and shares it with them, that they realize what is happening, WHO is happening . . . and then he's gone. They reflect on it: "Were not our hearts burning within us" when he was with us? They go back to Jerusalem to the other disciples and proclaim what they've experienced, as they hear of Peter's encounter with the risen Lord.

When a parish is in transition, it does feel like a journey. There's grief at the departure of the prior priest if it has been a good tenure and grief at dreams unfulfilled if it has not. There's concern about what the future might hold. There's worry about how one does this work of managing the parish and how one secures another priest.

But there will be moments of hearts strangely warmed, if the level of anxiety about this transition can be addressed honestly, appropriately, and prayerfully. God's will—not individual preference—will be the thing you seek. God is always doing a new thing (Isa. 43:19) and now God is doing a new thing with and for you and God's providence is sure. The wisdom of the great cloud of witnesses who have navigated this journey can inform you. May the best practices and tools contained in this book be a road map and a comfort as you journey.

Blessings,
The Rev. Dr. Mary Brennan Thorpe
Canon to the Ordinary
The Episcopal Diocese of Virginia

I

Introduction

The Structure of This Book

From Constancy and Peace . . .

It is a fact of life that those who live as part of a faith community see it as a constant in their lives. They know where it is, when it meets, what will happen there, and how the rhythm of the liturgy, the calendar, and the usual practices of the community shape the common life of the parish. It is, to many, a place of comfort and stability.

So what happens when the community is thrust out of that stability into a state of transition? What happens when the priest[1] departs?

. . . To Transition and Change

This book will walk you through the process of that time of transition step-by-step, with attention to the various roles of those who will be helping the parish find new leadership. It also recognizes that each parish is unique, and that one process doesn't fit all. Our intent is to help parishes seek God's will as they begin the next chapter of their story.

This work should be done efficiently, but not at the expense of time to hear the Holy Spirit's guidance. It is work that should be done in a way that recognizes that every voice in the parish matters and should be heard, but not every need can be met. It is work that names that parishes need clergy with different gifts at different times in their existence, and sometimes it is work that names uncomfortable truths with no easy answer.

---

1. The clergy leader may be titled rector, vicar, priest-in-charge, or some other title as designated by the bishop.

Transition is holy work. It is our prayer that this process will be spiritually transformative, not only for those who do the identified tasks of transition, but for the entire parish, as they are reminded of God's providence and God's habit of surprising us.

How to Read This Book

You will see sections addressed "For the Vestry," "For the Discernment Committee," and "For the Departing Priest." You are welcome to read any or all of it—vestry members are not forbidden from reading discernment committee chapters and vice versa!—but please understand that certain tasks are assigned to particular groups for a good reason.

There are variations in practices in each and every diocese in the Episcopal Church, because contexts differ and context matters. Your bishop, your canon to the ordinary, your transition ministry officer[2] are your best guides as to what are the practices and limitations and freedoms that are operative in your diocese. Trust them, follow their guidelines, and ask questions! This process, based on several years of doctoral research and several years of lived experience, has been a flexible and effective approach. Use it in partnership with your diocesan team and may it bring you the same excellent results we have experienced.

---

2. Note that with the exception of the bishop, titles for those who will assist you in your transition process vary based upon size of diocesan staff and specificity of roles. In some dioceses, there is a transition ministry officer with a title that mirrors that specific role. In other dioceses, the canon to the ordinary is your contact for all matters relating to transition processes. In a few dioceses, the bishop diocesan is also the transition officer. Check with your bishop's office to identify the key persons who will be assisting you.

II

---&---

A General Outline
of the Transition Process

In general, the normative process for transition is . . .

1. For the transition ministry office to have a conversation with the vestry, as soon as the priest's retirement/departure is announced, to discuss the road ahead, especially the vestry's role in the process and choices to be made.

2. For the church and priest to have a "good goodbye."

3. For the vestry to determine which model of transition process they will use, with the recommendation of the bishop and the diocesan staff who support transitions.

4. For the appropriate committee to be formed to carry out the next steps of transition.

5. For the vestry to vote on the finalist and, if affirmed, for the vestry to extend a call.

6. If the call is accepted, for the vestry and the candidate to negotiate the terms of call, set out in a letter of agreement.

7. For the candidate, the senior warden, and the bishop to sign the letter of agreement.

8. For a mutual ministry review to be conducted after the new priest has served for a year.

Rector Calls:

In the outline above, when you get to step 4, this is how the process proceeds:

- For a discernment committee to be constituted and commissioned.
- For the discernment committee to do the work of self-study[1] with the input of the congregation.
- For the discernment committee to publish a vestry- and bishop-approved community ministry portfolio, which provides an overview of the church and its vision.
- For the church to improve its website to include relevant and up-to-date information on the church and the search process, for the benefit of both potential candidates and potential parishioners.
- For the discernment committee to receive names and select a finalist after the Office of Transition Ministry vets the candidates.

Then the process goes forward as described in steps 5 through 9.

Priest-in-Charge Calls:

In some situations, it may be more appropriate for the parish to call a priest-in-charge rather than a rector. The only difference between the two calls is this: the priest-in-charge is appointed by the bishop for a time-limited term. In some cases, if the vestry requests it and the bishop concurs that this is a wise decision, the call can be changed to be an open-ended one, with no specific end date. In other words, this becomes a call to be rector.

From a practical standpoint, both priest-in-charge and rector have the same level of authority and responsibility as per the canons of the church. In our diocese, we recommend this process when the tenure of the departing priest has been relatively short and when the parish is generally healthy. We do *not* use it for parishes where the departing priest has had a

---

1. **Search Tools:** Tools that are used to complete this work, particularly in the self-study period, vary widely. Each vestry and each discernment committee are encouraged to work with the diocesan transition team in constructing a plan of action for their search process, either with or without an outside consultant. Much of this discovery results from self-study based on three questions: who have we been; who are we now; who is God calling us to be?

very long tenure, or when the departure has been occasioned by conflict or misconduct.

This model has an abbreviated self-study process, after which the bishop and the diocesan transition team assemble several pre-vetted and qualified candidates for the vestry's consideration. The vestry interviews and selects a candidate to request from the bishop. The most positive argument for calling a priest-in-charge is that it provides a long period of mutual discernment between parish and priest before making a more permanent call.

In this process, the parish cedes much control to the diocese to select potential candidates. The negative side to the priest-in-charge model is that priests may be reluctant to consider such a call, particularly if it involves moving, because there is no guarantee of continued employment beyond the term limit of the letter of agreement. The positive side is that it is a shorter process, does not require that the parish wait for the appointment of an available interim rector (usually the parish's liturgical and spiritual needs are attended to by a long-term supply priest), and that the parish does not have to adjust to a new priest in the form of an interim and then another new priest as their settled rector.

In the outline of the process above, here's what happens in step 4: The vestry decides if they want to create a mini-discernment team, an ad hoc group to do a small self-study[2] that helps shape a list of gifts/skills/qualities that would serve the parish well in their next chapter, or if the vestry wants to do that task themselves. If the parish is small, this is a manageable task for the vestry. If it is not, the vestry will appreciate delegating that task. This team—and use of a term like "team" emphasizes the distinction between what had always been called the search committee and something much briefer and more focused—does the brief self-study to develop that list, gives it to the diocesan transition team to seek candidates, and interviews the small group of candidates that the diocesan transition team gives them. Thereafter, the process continues from step 5 above.

---

2. An earlier version of this process did not include the mini-self-study. We have found, though, that it is wise to invite parishioners to voice their opinions about what is needed, not only to give them a voice in the process, but to see if there are any issues that were not known to the lay leadership that might require different gifts or some preliminary work with the congregation before continuing.

Alternative Processes

If a vestry wishes to consider an alternative process, such as beginning a search prior to the incumbent's departure, this would generally require the approval of the bishop. This is not a process that should be presented by the departing priest. The vestry must present its plan and reasoning behind that plan to the bishop via the transition ministry officer.

- There should not be a nonstandard process if the departure of the incumbent is due to misconduct or serious conflict or if the incumbent's tenure has ended due to death or to a serious physical or emotional disability.

- The calling of a new priest after an incumbent completes a particularly long tenure usually requires a standard process, but in rare cases an exception may be made. Again, it is the *vestry's* responsibility to make the case and it is the bishop's prerogative, in conversation with the vestry, to define the nature of the process.

Remember that this is not a hiring process, it is a process of discernment about a covenantal relationship. As we approach this, it is wise to remember the words of the priest and theologian Henri Nouwen, who describes discernment thus:

> Christian discernment is not the same as decision making. Reaching a decision can be straightforward: we consider our goals and options; maybe we list the pros and cons of each possible choice; and then we choose the action that meets our goal most effectively. Discernment, on the other hand, is about listening and responding to that place within us where our deepest desires align with God's desire. As discerning people, we sift through our impulses, motives, and options to discover which ones lead us closer to divine love and compassion for ourselves and other people and which ones lead us further away.
>
> Discernment reveals new priorities, directions, and gifts from God. We come to realize that what previously seemed so important for our lives loses its power over us. Our desire to be successful, well liked and influential becomes increasingly less important as we move closer to God's heart.

To our surprise, we even may experience a strange inner freedom to follow a new call or direction as previous concerns move into the background of our consciousness. We begin to see the beauty of the small and hidden life that Jesus lived in Nazareth. Most rewarding of all is the discovery that as we pray more each day, God's will—that is, God's concrete ways of loving us and our world—gradually is made known to us. [3]

---

3. Henri Nouwen, *Discernment: Reading the Signs of Daily Life* (New York: HarperOne, 2013), 17.

III

---◈---

FOR THE DEPARTING PRIEST

It sounds trite to say that leaving a parish is hard, but it is important to acknowledge that. Even if one's tenure has been difficult, we form relationships with those whom we serve. Even if we have not accomplished everything we had hoped for, we know we have affected the lives of people in the parish and in the community. Even if we have been longing for the freedom of retirement, we wonder how our identity will reshape itself without the quotidian work of parish life.

A departing priest may be tempted to push down the feelings of grief attendant with the ending of a pastoral relationship, filling the last days of our tenure with activities and projects. It is perhaps our denial of the finitude of things, of our own mortality, of our sense that we didn't accomplish everything that we wished we had.

Still, it is a necessary thing to do.

Your parishioners are working through a range of feelings themselves. You've seen this before as you've pastored them through their own griefs. They may present as scared, anxious, uncertain, angry, stressed. The thoughts that run through their minds range from, "What if there is no priest to comfort me and to eulogize me when I die?" to "She would have to leave now right in the middle of the building project/personnel restructuring/introduction to a new stewardship campaign/illness of the organist." Those who may have been less enthusiastic about your ministry are now facing the reality that, to paraphrase the words of a former president, they won't have you to kick around anymore. Lay leaders wonder what burdens will be placed upon them, and if they are up to the task.

Thoughts may be running through your head as well. "I really do need to leave, but maybe I should stay a little longer, since we've had construction delays on the new building." "I'm exhausted, but they seem so unready for a search." "If I go, then that difficult person may believe that he has defeated me." "If I had one more year, I might have been able to [you fill in the blank]."

And in the midst of it, you are also dealing with your own discomfort with people saying how wonderful you've been, how they cannot imagine the parish without you, expressing their gratitude for your service and love, telling you laudatory stories that you had long ago forgotten. Most of us are a little uneasy when we are the subject of praise, and the last few months of your tenure will be filled with that.

So here are some realities, strategies, ideas for you in the time before you depart your parish:

- Remember that transition processes have evolved since the last time you were called, and the diocesan transition ministry officer is actually very aware of the fact that every parish is unique and every process has its particular joys and challenges. This means that you cannot try to control or influence that process. You do not have a role in the selection of an interim. Neither do you have a role in proposing a particular transition methodology for the parish. Trust that your bishop and your diocesan transition ministry officer have that covered.

- If the vestry has an idea and wishes to propose something to your bishop and your diocesan transition ministry officer, it is their responsibility to do so, not yours. They should be aware, however, that your bishop knows what works, what doesn't work and why, and has the authority to direct the lay leadership to preserve "the order, discipline, and unity" of the diocese.

- Think ahead joyfully! Plan a vacation for the time immediately after your last day. You can visit grandchildren, go to the beach, go to Paris— you've earned it, and so has your spouse, if you are so blessed. Time to unhook from the place you've served, and it's easier to unhook if you are not reachable.

- Complete whatever materials your diocese requires to ensure a smooth hand-off. If this is not a part of the process in your diocese, you might put together some key priest-to-priest information about matters like works in process, key players, pastoral issues. This document will provide a way for the interim or priest-in-charge that follows to "hit the ground running" and will assure that important information, particularly the sort of information that a priest conveys to another priest, doesn't slip through the cracks. If you have questions about what to include, remember the last time you were called to serve a parish. What did you wish someone had told you? That's what your successor will want to know.

- Now is the time to do some coaching of your lay leadership. If you have always run the vestry meetings, you might want to coach your wardens in how you construct an agenda, how you manage different viewpoints, how you make sure there is always a spiritual "heart" to the work that you do together. You might also coach ordained and lay staff to take on more responsibility in their areas. Remember that they will be anxious too. Your transition ministry officer can meet with them, if you've got more than a couple of part-timers. Know that we do not require blanket resignations, which was a practice a long time ago.

- You'll also want to coach the parish as a whole on what you will and will not do in terms of interacting with them after your departure. Most dioceses have a policy guideline for resigning priests, and we recommend that you familiarize yourself with it as well as sharing it with your vestry, and in a more informal manner, with your parishioners. The intent is not to exclude you from the life of the parish you have served so much as to leave graceful space for your successor to develop relationships with parishioners without your presence in the system as a "shadow pastor." You will have done your job of saying goodbye well when you can see from afar that they have bonded well with their new priest. Keep in mind that one's role as a parish priest is to serve as a guide and companion for one section of their pilgrimage, after which they are handed off to the next guide and companion, who will bring different but equally important gifts. Only God serves as their companion for the entire journey, and that is more than enough.

- Be gracious if the parish wants to give you a parting gift, or dedicate a project or space to your ministry among them. Even if you hate to have people say complimentary things about you, let them have that opportunity. If there are old wounds that need healing, attend to them. Forgiveness (both asking and offering) is a beautiful parting gift.

- Make sure that all the necessary passwords or administrator log-ins have been identified for the lay leadership, all keys have been turned in, and any church credit card has been returned. Similarly, any church records or documents or files that are in your desk at home need to come back to the church, appropriately filed. If you have lived in a rectory, please clean it out as you would any apartment or home you are vacating. If there are things in the rectory that need fixing, make sure whomever is in charge of buildings and grounds in the parish is aware.

Postdeparture (for retiring priests):

- If you are moving to a new community, make sure that you give your new contact information to your diocesan offices, and if you are moving out of your diocese, do let your new diocese know that you're there, whether you want to be available for supply work/interim work/consulting work or not.

- If you are not moving to a new community, find another parish in which to worship. This may mean spending a few months attending in a variety of churches to find one that feels like a fit. Do not assume that you will have a priestly role in that place; some rectors want that and some do not. Do not automatically assume that a large parish is your best option. Particularly if you want to continue to share your priestly gifts in a helpful way, you could be a great gift to a smaller parish with a solo priest. If that is the case, make sure mutual expectations are clear. One priest we know does not want to preach anymore, but loves to preside, so the vocational deacon or the seminarian in that parish preaches when he presides. One loves to do visitations to the homebound, but no longer wants to preside or preach because of physical limitations. One simply sits in the pews. There is no one model—it's what you want and feel called to do and what the rector/vicar/priest-in-charge feels is a good fit.

- Do remember that, if you are married, this is the first time in a long time that you and your spouse get to worship side by side. Enjoy that blessing!

IV

FOR THE VESTRY: PHASE ONE

Vestry Involvement in the Process: A Quick View from 10,000 Feet

Initial Steps

- Contact your bishop's office to set up an initial meeting with transition ministry officer and/or one of the bishops.
- Notify the transition ministry officer of the priest's last day, and last day on payroll, if it is different.
- Plan appropriate goodbye activities for the departing priest and family.
- Engage supply clergy to cover Sundays/pastoral care after departure of the priest while the vestry determines what transition process is appropriate for the parish, in consultation with the diocesan transition team.[1]
- Choose the appropriate transition process with the advice and consent of the bishop and/or the bishop's staff.

Next Steps in the Interim Rector Model (Traditional Process)

- Retain an interim rector with the guidance of the transition ministry officer.
- Engage a supply priest, if necessary, to cover worship services and pastoral emergencies until the interim rector begins.

---

1. Often there is an initial meeting between the vestry and the transition ministry officer to determine the process prior to the departure of the priest. In this case, there may be very little gap between the departure of the incumbent and the arrival of an interim. Check with your transition ministry officer to see if this will apply for your parish.

- Select and appoint members of the search committee and designate a chair of the discernment committee, with input from transition ministry officer on how to select the committee.
- Approve a budget for the discernment committee. Your transition ministry officer should have guidelines for what is usual.
- Wardens should periodically meet with the chair of the discernment committee.
- Be sure that the parish pledge to the diocese, clergy benefits (pension, insurance, etc.), parish audits, parochial reports, and other records are up-to-date as the search process begins.
- Create a compensation package for the new rector at the request of the discernment committee (see page 148).
- Approve the community ministry portfolio before submission to your transition minister so it may be posted to the national database (*www. otmportfolio.org*).

Extending a Call—Interim Rector Process

- Receive the name of the recommended candidate from the discernment committee.
- Invite the candidate to meet the vestry.
- Decide whether or not to affirm the recommendation of the discernment committee. If yes, issue the call to the candidate.
- Negotiate the letter of agreement with the incoming rector.
- Plan a celebration for the discernment committee.
- Wish your interim rector well and celebrate their ministry with you.
- Welcome the new rector (and family, if applicable) to the parish.

Next Steps—Priest-in-Charge Model

- Engage a long-term supply priest who will support the parish as you carry out your process. Be clear with the supply priest what your expectations are: Sunday worship, pastoral calls on an on-call basis, staff management, vestry involvement. The first two are essential; the second two are optional based upon your needs.

- If the vestry delegates responsibility for the brief self-study and/or interviewing of candidates to a discernment team,[2] they should designate a chair of the discernment team and name its members, with input from your transition ministry officer on how to select the committee.
- Schedule periodic meetings of wardens and team leader.
- Be sure that the parish pledge to the diocese, clergy benefits (pension, insurance, etc.); parish audits, parochial reports, and other records are up-to-date as the search process begins.
- Create compensation package for new priest-in-charge (see page 148).
- Approve a summary of the qualities/gifts/skills that would be desired in the new priest-in-charge and transmit it to the transition ministry officer.

Extending a Call—Priest-in-Charge Process

- Receive the name of the candidate from the discernment team.
- Invite the candidate to meet the vestry.
- If the vestry agrees with the recommendation, issue the call to the candidate.
- Negotiate the letter of agreement with the incoming priest-in-charge, with guidance from your transition ministry officer and your bishop. These are tripartite agreements because the bishop appoints a priest-in-charge, unlike rector calls, so clarity between all parties is especially important.
- Plan a celebration for your discernment team.
- Welcome the new priest-in-charge (and family, if applicable) to the parish.

---

2. This group is given a different title to distinguish between the more intensive and formal work that the discernment committee does, which might involve a variety of tools of self-study and discernment. The team's involvement is focused and limited in scope.

Throughout the Process

Pray for the parish, vestry, committee, and candidates.

But What Happened to the Parish Profile?

If you have prior experience of searches for clergy in the past, you have undoubtedly noticed that there is no discussion of the document known as the "parish profile." This document was usually anywhere from ten to forty pages, included pictures of what the parish was most proud of, had a lengthy history of the parish, and described all the ministries that were active. It also described the priest the parish was seeking.

It was a useful tool in the days before the internet. It gave a lot of information in one place and served as a marketing document for the position. Priests requested a copy, received it by mail, and decided whether or not they would send their material by mail back to the parish. There was a certain sameness to all of these documents: "We're a friendly and welcoming church!" "Our youth group is lively!" "We seek someone who will help us grow!" That sometimes made it difficult for candidates to discern what the parish really was looking for or needed. And if you talk to parishioners who served on search committees that developed such profiles, they will tell you that the most exhausting, tedious, and mind-numbing part of the process was the development of the profile, which often added six months onto the process and was marked by pitched battles over which picture to use and whether or not the Oxford comma was anathema.

Information sharing is very different these days. The moment your priest announces their retirement or that they are taking a new call, potential candidates are already looking at your website to learn about your parish. What kinds of activities do they see? What do the pictures of the parish tell about who you are and how you operate? How many groups like AA or the Scouts meet in your building? Are there mission and outreach activities going on? Does the very long webpage about your history suggest that you're more interested in focusing on your past than on your present or future? Why would you want to invest a lot of time and effort on writing your story for a single-use document when you can upgrade/update your website, which may be one of the most potent tools for attracting newcomers?

Much of what used to reside in parish profiles—perhaps 90 percent—already lives (or should live) on your website. It may not contain everything, but it is a dynamic tool both for evangelism and for telling your story. The balance of your story—your parish by the numbers, how you operate as a faith community—will be told in the community ministry portfolio. In the meantime, though, consider your website. If it's summertime and the home page still shows the calendar for Holy Week, that's a problem. If someone cannot figure out when and where your services are within five seconds, that's a problem. Ask your transition ministry officer to point out some effective websites for parishes of your size and resources to use as models.

So do not mourn the passing of the parish profile. It served its purpose. Now there are tools that are more effective and more oriented to the way candidates research potential calls, and that's a good thing.

Planning a "Good Goodbye"

Occasionally, there is a tendency to want to leap right into the work of replacing your departing priest. While this is natural, particularly for those who are very goal-oriented, it's not yet time.

First, you need to say goodbye.

If you deny the grief that you feel in losing a beloved spiritual companion, it can hamper the work of healing. If you short-circuit that work, the parish can become "stuck" in trying to imagine God's will for the parish in the future and what gifts and skills their next priest should bring.

If the relationship with the incumbent priest has become painful, you still need to have a "good goodbye." In some ways, you need it even more, because parishes grieve the loss of dreams they had had for the years when things were not going well.

Nevertheless, saying goodbye is a necessary and healthy way to end a relationship.

Different parishes find different ways to say goodbye. Some plan a series of small gatherings at parishioners' homes. Some plan a major party. We've seen some gifts to departing rectors like these:

- a "purse," a monetary gift gathered by a special collection,
- a gift honoring a special thing the departing priest is planning on doing or loves (one parish gave their priest a kayak!),
- dedication of some improvement to the parish if the priest has no need of funds and would prefer to be honored in this way. One parish upgraded the walkway to their memorial garden, since the priest had labored so faithfully to care for dying parishioners and did not want any monetary gift or object.

Other parishes gathered notes and stories into a binder to share with the priest because there were lots of cherished memories to be shared.

The final service is usually quite emotional for all. We are a liturgical people, though, and this service is part of processing the grief and preparing for the new beginning. It is appropriate to include all or a portion of the rite entitled "A Service for the Ending of a Pastoral Relationship and Leave-Taking from a Congregation," found on page 339 in the *Book of Occasional Services*, as a way of marking the end of that chapter of the parish's and the priest's story.

Options for Calls: A Closer Look

There are two primary options for transitioning to new clergy leadership, as described in the overview on pages 3–7.

The first is the one that is traditional:

- calling an interim rector,
- commissioning a discernment committee who will do the work of self-study of the parish, development of descriptive materials about the call, advertising the position, due diligence, winnowing of initial candidates, interviews, site visits, local interviews, and recommendation of the final candidate to the vestry,

- meeting with and assessing whether or not to affirm the recommendation of the discernment committee,
- issuing a call and negotiating a letter of agreement, with the consent of the bishop.

The second one, priest-in-charge, is becoming more common:

- arranging for supply clergy for the shorter period of time that this process will take,
- deciding on the primary gifts/skills that are needed in the parish's next priest,
- receiving pre-vetted candidates from the transition ministry officer,
- having either the entire vestry or a subset of it interview candidates to discern if the gifts/skills align with what the parish needs,
- issuing a call and negotiating a letter of agreement, with the consent of the bishop.

The primary difference between the two is that the PIC call is time-limited. The LOA is usually for three years, with the possibility of conversion to rectorship if all is well after eighteen months. The priest-in-charge does much of the same work as an interim, including making necessary changes to processes, staff, programs, and worship, in consultation with the vestry. It is akin to a long engagement before the marriage.

The upside to the PIC model is that it is somewhat faster, usually six months or so depending on the season of the year[3] and the particularities of the parish's context. The downside is that the parish cedes much more control to the diocesan staff and deals with a smaller pool of candidates, sometimes as few as two.

The upside to the traditional interim model is that a priest with specialized training will attend to any necessary changes, and has the freedom to do what may turn out to be difficult things without worrying that it will

---

3. During the busiest liturgical seasons such as Advent/Christmas and Lent/Easter, priests and parishes are focused upon the rites and rituals of those seasons, and the ability to focus on a transition process is difficult, both for priest and committee.

impact the priest's ability to take the permanent call. It frees the new permanent priest to focus on building relationships rather than doing "parish housekeeping work" that might step on a few toes. The downside is that it takes longer, between twelve and eighteen months.

In some cases, the bishop will require that a parish follow a particular approach, especially in situations of conflict or of a painful parting with the prior rector. Generally, however, it is the vestry's choice which approach they prefer.

A more detailed discussion of the role of the vestry in the priest-in-charge model follows on page 22.

Securing an Interim

The interim rector is a priest who is specifically trained to do the work of preparing a congregation for their next "settled priest." In most dioceses, the interim cannot be a candidate for the permanent position. Candidates to be interim for a parish are usually recommended to the vestry by the transition ministry officer. Most TMOs endeavor to provide more than one candidate whose gifts match the needs of the parish, but given the present shortage in gifted interims, it is sometimes a challenge to present more than one candidate. The vestry meets with the candidate(s) and then requests that their chosen candidate be appointed by the bishop. Occasionally these are priests who have retired from permanent positions but want to continue to serve the church. If they are retired, the approval of the Church Pension Group may also be a prerequisite for certain calls.

Interims usually begin their work a few weeks after the departing rector has left. It is wise for the parish to have a little breathing room before the interim comes on board. Interim rector letters of agreement usually specify that the term of the agreement is until the new rector has been called, although in rare circumstances, they may dictate otherwise.

Their client—and this may come as a surprise to the parish—is NOT the parish, although the parish pays their compensation. It is actually the next permanent priest. In essence, their task is to address issues that need to be addressed, to attend to any clean-up necessary (either literally or figuratively) in partnership with the vestry, so that the parish is ready to welcome their next priest in great condition administratively and spiritually. The letter of agreement[4] states the mutual goals and expectations thus:

I. Preamble for Specific Interim Goals

Goals of the Interim Ministry period: The interim rector shall work closely with the wardens, vestry, staff, and other parish leaders toward the major goal which is to prepare the congregation for the coming of the next rector. The primary work is summarized as follows:

- *Help the congregation deal with any present feelings or residual issues from the previous years or the recent rector's departure;*
- *Deal with internal conflicts when present and help heal any divisions within the congregation;*
- *Help the vestry and lay leaders bring about such change, if needed, to align parish life and administration to affirm the values of the parish and meet the generally accepted standards in the diocese.*

Other goals of the interim period are the nationally recognized five developmental tasks during the interim period in supporting a healthy congregational life:

1. *Assisting the congregation in dealing with its recent history;*
2. *Seeking and discovering an identity for the future with a new rector;*
3. *Continuing to affirm the present leadership while including new emerging leaders;*
4. *Strengthening the relationship with the diocese; and, as the interim period draws to a close,*
5. *Committing itself to a new future of mutual ministry with the new rector.*

The vestry and interim rector agree to work closely together and to support each other by prayer, word, and example to achieve these goals. They will also provide time for mutual ministry reviews when they shall discuss

---

4. This sample letter of agreement is the template used in the Diocese of Virginia. Other dioceses have their own version of this, but the naming of these goals for the interim's work is usually a feature of such letters.

and mutually review the total ministry of the parish on a regular basis in order to intentionally:

1. *Provide them each an opportunity to assess how well they are fulfilling their responsibilities to each other and to the ministry they share.*

2. *Determine progress on the specific interim ministry goals and adjust or change them as needed.*

3. *Recognize, affirm, and celebrate the parishioners' shared ministry by including the congregation in the education and ongoing evaluation of these goals.*

4. *Isolate areas of conflict or disappointment which have not received adequate attention and which may be adversely affecting mutual ministry.*

5. *Clarify expectation of all parties to help put any future conflicts in manageable form.*

6. *Plan healthy closure for the interim ministry and prepare for the coming of the next rector.*

If desirable a mutually agreed upon third party may be engaged to facilitate any steps in the Mutual Ministry Review process.[5]

Calling a Priest-in-Charge Rather Than Using an Interim Rector

First, an explanation of the title "priest-in-charge" may be helpful. The priest-in-charge functions in every way as rector, except the priest-in-charge does not have the tenure of a rector. The tenure of the priest-in-charge is for a negotiated period (normally three years). In many dioceses, after a minimum period of eighteen months, and a careful review of mutual ministry between the vestry and the priest-in-charge, the vestry makes a determination as to whether or not it wishes to elect the priest-in-charge as rector.

---

5. The work and goals of interims during the time of transition, cited here in italics, were originally laid out in Loren Mead's *A Change of Pastors and How It Affects the Congregation*, rev. ed. (Herndon, VA: Rowman & Littlefield, 2012) 18. They are usually included in letters of agreement between the congregation, the interim rector, and the bishop.

If election of priest-in-charge as rector is not desired by the vestry, or if the priest-in-charge does not accept the call, the vestry then enters into a standard search process. As with interim rectors, the priest-in-charge serves at the pleasure of the bishop. One common model of the relationship between the congregation and the priest-in-charge is that the relationship may be ended by a majority vote of the vestry, with sixty days' notice; by resignation of the priest-in-charge, with sixty days' notice; or by decision of the bishop.

The Process

The vestry selects a long-term supply priest, with assistance from the bishop's office. The vestry appoints members of the priest-in-charge discernment team. This can be populated by a subset of members of the vestry or other parishioners.

Self-Discovery/Self-Definition

This group creates criteria and expectations for ministry of the priest-in-charge (mutual ministry description), usually using a congregational tool such as the "Appreciative Inquiry Congregational Meeting"[6] to identify key gifts or qualities or skills the new priest might bring. This approach provides an opportunity for parishioners to share their thoughts about the future of the parish. It is usually structured in such a way that the focus is on what the priest brings to the community, not about age, gender, orientation, ethnicity, marital status, or other external descriptors.

Candidate Evaluation

The team chooses the sequence of candidate evaluation steps: scheduling initial interviews, questions for conversations, correspondence templates, candidate research, etc. They receive a list of candidates' names from the bishop's office, with pertinent materials such as Office of Transition Ministry (OTM) profiles, resumes, comments. These candidates have been pre-vetted.

---

6. See this tool on page 133.

The team begins candidate evaluation process: review of candidate materials, sermons, Skype/phone conversations, etc.

As they have greater clarity about the candidates, they might also visit candidates in their own ministry setting. Ultimately, the team selects the recommended candidate. Depending on your diocese's practice, there might be additional vetting to be completed before the call can be made. Check with your diocesan transition ministry officer.

Selecting a Discernment Committee and Committee Chair

The vestry selects the discernment committee and commissions them to do their work. The committee consists of between five and nine people and should not have members of the vestry serving on it, though this may be unavoidable for some smaller parishes. You should look for particular qualities and skills in selecting search committee members. These are listed below. You will also be selecting the committee chair. We recommend against the group selecting their chair from within. Often this results in the most dominant personality being elected rather than the person who has gifts for facilitation. Many vestries choose the chair first, and then come up with a list of possible candidates to review with the chair prior to contacting them to see if they have an interest in serving. While this is not required, it appears to support a good result.

Frequently, parishioners will volunteer themselves before you are ready to make choices. Sometimes these are people who served on a prior search committee. These people may be problematic despite their past experience if they are wedded to a particular approach that does not align with the way transitions are done today. You can tell them, or any others who have volunteered prior to your vestry meeting to select the committee, that while their gifts are well-known to you, there is no guarantee they will be asked to serve given the limited number of persons who can fulfill this role, and that even if they are not on the committee, there will be much other important work to do.

Guard against the desire to use participation on the committee as a reward for past services rendered, or as a way to keep a parishioner engaged who lately seems to be drifting away from the church. Even more important, if your sense is that a person has a particular agenda for this transition, they should not be a part of this committee.[7]

One method that greatly relies on the work of the Holy Spirit has been used in many vestries with surprisingly excellent results. The vestry is told that they will be expected to come back for their next meeting with four names of people who would fulfill the qualities that make for a good member of the committee. They should pray about parishioners who might be the right ones for this important and sensitive work, but not discuss it with other vestry members or parishioners. They should not ask the people whose names come to them in prayer whether they would serve. That will come later. Then, at the next meeting, the vestry members are asked to write the names of the people they thought of, each on one post-it note. One person stands and says "I think John Doe would be good" and places her sticky note with John Doe's name on it on the wall. Any other persons who also thought of John Doe add their sticky notes to the first one. The next person stands and says "I think Marva Smith would be good," places the sticky note with Marva's name on the wall, anyone else who thought of Marva adds their sticky note, and so on. Remarkably, the prayers and discernment of the group often give a list of top candidates who meet the needs of the work in very short order. This was done most memorably in a large vestry that always struggled to make decisions because of the brilliance and argumentative nature of its members, and they came up with a list of eleven names in fifteen minutes. They had a few extras in case any of the top of the list could not commit to the work, but the combined list met and exceeded all the qualities that a vestry should seek for members of the committee.

---

7. In one particularly tragic case, someone was put on a discernment committee who desperately wanted the parish to call a particular priest with whom the person had a prior pastoral relationship. The person somehow wangled the chairmanship of the committee, never revealing the prior relationship. The call fell apart when the priest, encouraged by the chair, insisted on a compensation package far greater than the published available compensation. The lack of trust and pain in this situation had widespread impact.

Qualities Desired in All Members

Time:

A typical transition process runs about twelve to eighteen months from the time a rector leaves to the time the next rector is on board. If members cannot commit to regular meetings and prioritize this work, it will slow down the process and hamper good discernment.

Gifts for Discernment:

Discernment is essentially "Holy Analysis." It means being a good listener, being able to hold one's opinions lightly, to be able to spend time in prayer and measured discussion. Besides time, this is the most essential quality.

Representative of a Cross-Section of the Parish:

Discernment committees should be young and old, new and longtime members, of different backgrounds, and with different experiences of the church . . . but not "single-issue voters."

Discretion:

Members need to be able to keep information confidential, especially information about the applicants.

Courage and Kindness:

Serving on a discernment committee is rewarding work, but it can be taxing. The members of the committee represent the hope for the future of the parish, but they can also be the objects of misdirected anxiety. Committee members should be able to hear criticism without feeling the need to "people please" or getting defensive.

Additional Helpful Skills

Project Management, Organization:

Giving proper attention to goals, timetables, and how each member will use their gifts and skills.

Public Speaking:

One member, possibly the chair, should be able to inform and/or motivate the parish.

Tech Savvy:

At least one member should understand the basics of web design and electronic communication.

Writing and Storytelling:

The final product of the self-study work will essentially be a storytelling document based on lots of conversation with and information about the congregation and community. Look for members who can turn the information and conversation into a defining narrative.

However, discernment committee members with these skills must first have time, and gifts for discernment. The committee can always enlist outside help for the more technical aspects of their work; it's more important that members can commit themselves to the work and discern.

What Is the Work of the Discernment Committee?

Just to remind you as you prepare to select your discernment committee, here are the basics:

They Will Build a Map of the Past, Present, and Future

- Discern where the parish has been, where it is today, and where God is calling it to be in the future.
- See what kinds of gifts and graces are already present at the parish that can move it to where God is calling it to be.
- Identify those gifts and skills the parish will need in your next rector (augmenting what you've already got) to assist you in that process.

This is practical, information-gathering work; it is also spiritual discernment work. Depending on the practices of your diocese, your discernment committee may use a diocese-recommended consultant or they may choose to do it all themselves. Most parish discernment committees can do this work on their own.

They Will Draw the Map for Candidates to Understand Where Your Future Lies

They will build a body of information that identifies the gifts and graces the parish needs from the next rector, based upon what they've discovered, what the dreams, hopes, and aspirations are for the parish, and what the challenges ahead may be. This will feed the community ministry portfolio that will be posted on the Episcopal Church database and will be accessed by potential candidates. This document, in partnership with your website, will invite candidates into conversation with you as you mutually discern if there is a fit.

They Will Choose the Parish's Coauthor for the Next Chapter of Your Story

The discernment committee will assess the applications of those who seek to serve as the next rector. The idea is to see if the gifts and graces they offer match the parish's needs. They also should see who has the right chemistry to do well in your parish, to get you to where God is leading you next. The discernment committee will seek "The One": the person to whom the Holy Spirit has led them. The discernment committee will recommend this candidate to you, the vestry, who will meet with the person and their family and will vote on whether this is your next rector. Your bishop and transition ministry officer will have a part in this as well, assisting in the vetting process and giving final approval of the call.

The Commissioning of a Discernment Committee

When the vestry has organized a discernment committee to seek nominees and candidates for a position opening in a congregation, it is important to publicly recognize and commission the members of the committee for this sacred ministry. The following is a form that may be used or adapted for the blessing and commission of the committee. The commissioning should take place at a Sunday liturgy. This form is written to fit in with Prayers of the People during the Eucharist. In cases where this is used, it is recommended to omit the Confession of Sin for that liturgy. This allows us to end the Liturgy of the Word with the commissioning and the Peace.

At the end of the prayers of the people, the senior warden comes to the crossing in the church building and faces the people. Members of the discernment committee stand in the aisle facing the warden.

> *Junior Warden or other Parish Official:* I present to you these persons to be installed as members of the discernment committee in this congregation.
>
> *Senior Warden:* God will not overlook your work and the love which you show for his sake.
>
> Teach me to do what pleases you, for you are my God:
>
> *Committee Members:* Let your good Spirit lead me on level ground.
>
> *Senior Warden:* As members of the discernment committee, you are hereby charged to diligently search for a candidate to be the next rector/vicar of _____ Church, _____, Diocese of X. You are given the authority to act as a subcommittee of the vestry and to rely upon the services and resources of the Diocese of X, seeking the guidance of the Holy Spirit to bring a call to the vestry. As members of this congregation, know that we will pray for you and give you the support necessary to fulfill your charge. May God, who has given you the ability to fulfill this ministry, give you the grace to accomplish it.
>
> *Celebrant:* Let us pray. (A period of prolonged silence is kept for private prayer.) Regard, O Lord, our supplications, and confirm with your heavenly benediction your servants whom we admit today to this ministry; that with sincere devotion of mind and body they may offer you a service acceptable to your divine Majesty; through Jesus Christ our Lord. Amen.
>
> In the Name of God and of this congregation, and on behalf of the vestry, I commission you as the discernment committee for _____ Church. In the Name of the Father, and of the Son, and of the Holy Spirit. AMEN.
>
> (*The Celebrant continues the worship with the Peace.*)

V

OTHER VESTRY CONSIDERATIONS

Communications during the Time of Transition

It is a good practice to have regular "check-in" meetings between the wardens and the chair(s) of the discernment committee, focused primarily on progress in the steps of transition. We would also suggest that there be periodic meetings of the chair(s) and the whole vestry, particularly if the process is leading to work that requires participation of the whole congregation (surveys, focus groups, "town hall meetings"). This is useful because it is an opportunity to flag communication needs, resource needs, or rough spots that would benefit from the wisdom of the vestry. It also provides the opportunity to make presentations about progress such as survey or focus group results and draft responses to the narrative questions in the community ministry portfolio.

Some discernment committees use their vestry as a sounding board if there might be challenging questions to ask parishioners.

The vestry will need to provide some data to the discernment committee, such as what the compensation package for the next priest will look like. The vestry will also need to review and approve the content of the community ministry portfolio prior to its publication.

"Where we are in the process" updates, either published in the parish newsletter or bulletin, or presented during announcement time during services, remind parishioners that things are happening even if those things aren't visible to them.

It is a useful thing for the discernment committee to present an adult forum talking about what has been published to promote the position in the community ministry portfolio. Generally, we recommend that this revolve around the answers to the narrative questions rather than the nuts and bolts of the numbers.

It's important to share enough information that everyone has a sense of forward motion in the process, but there is some information that requires COMPLETE CONFIDENTIALITY.

When you start to receive applications from prospective candidates, you can say NOTHING about candidates. Not the number of applications, not whether Father Fred applied, not whether there are any women candidates, not where applicants come from. NOTHING, not even to your nearest and dearest.

Your response to any inquiry about these things is "we are not allowed to share any of those details, and I'm sure you wouldn't want me to compromise the process by sharing confidential information. Please keep us in prayer as we discern God's will for our beloved parish."

One more thing: often parishioners will approach you with ideas for candidates. Because we want a level playing field for all candidates, here's a graceful to handle it: say "Thank you so much for telling me about Father Fred. Once our parish's community ministry portfolio is up on the national database, please do encourage your daughter's brother-in-law's priest to review it and discern whether or not they feel called to discern with us. We'll let everyone know when it's posted!" In other words, the burden is on the parishioner to reach out to Father Fred, not on the discernment committee. Frequently, such priests have no interest in making a move at this time, and it is their decision whether or not they want to apply. If that parishioner asks if Father Fred applied, you say, "All those who discerned they wanted to apply have applied, and I'm afraid I am not permitted to tell you whether or not he is among them. But we know that the Holy Spirit will guide us all, both the candidates and the discernment committee, as we work together to fulfill God's will."[1]

---

1. A lesson in trying to go around the Holy Spirit: a committee aggressively pursued a candidate whom someone on the committee had heard about. The priest definitely had some of the skills they were looking for, but did not have others that were important to congregational life. He told them

Lastly, many parishes choose to have a page on their website relating to the search process. It usually does not contain a link to your parish's community ministry portfolio in the Episcopal Church database, since all priests know where to find that. It might, however, point to information about the community, updates on the search process, and other such information. This is yet another place where your prayer for discernment might be published.

Staff Issues

In some dioceses in the past, there was a practice of requiring all staff to submit their resignation letters upon the departure of the rector, to be kept in the desk of the rector. When the new rector came, they could choose which resignations to accept and which to hold. The result of that practice was uncertainty in the hearts of staffers and parishioners, grief when a beloved staffer was dismissed, and a lack of continuity. The church now understands that this is unhealthy.

It *is* the responsibility of the cleric to select and manage the staff, be they lay or ordained. That said, we have learned that it is unhelpful for there to be a wholesale dismissal of staff. One of the tasks of the interim period is to address any personnel issues that have not been well addressed by the previous rector. We recommend to interim rectors that they consult with the vestry regarding these matters and jointly develop a plan to remediate the issues or to dismiss the employee. State employment law in your jurisdiction may have a say about personnel issues, particularly on matters such as age discrimination. But we hold ourselves to a higher standard as the church. We hope that any outstanding personnel issues can be addressed with

---

several times, clearly and unambiguously, that he was happy where he was and had no desire to discern with him. They continued to press him. He was flattered by this attention, and started to consider the call. They had, in many ways, decided that he was the right fit before they got to know him. He thought that their interest in him might be the Holy Spirit at play in an unusual way. He was called to the parish. It wasn't a good fit for them or for him, and although he is serving faithfully and to the best of his abilities, he is not happy in the call. With the exception of some of the committee members, parishioners have not warmed to him and are unhappy with some of his preferences in leadership style and in liturgical practice. Everyone is working to make the best of it, particularly the priest, but this is not the ideal outcome.

compassion, with encouragement, and with clarity of expectations. If the only option is to dismiss an employee, we expect the vestry and the interim rector to do this with as much kindness as is possible.

On occasion, an assistant or associate rector remains in the parish when the rector leaves. Sometimes the assistant or associate leaves during the time of transition. Sometimes they stay throughout and even after the time of transition. If we remember that the ordained employees also report to the rector, we can understand that it may be the choice of the assistant or associate to leave when the new rector begins. This is normal: assistants and associates usually only stay at one parish for a few years before seeking a rectorship of their own. When this happens, this does not mean that the new rector is "driving our beloved assistant out" or that there is cause to be unhappy with the new rector. It simply means that those who serve the church do many things in the course of their vocation, and that from time to time they feel God calling them to do something new.

One last thought: often parishes that have an assistant want their assistant to become their next rector. This is not the policy of most dioceses, for a very specific reason: the role of rector and the role of assistant are very different. The rector often has to do the hard things, the managerial tasks, that may challenge people. The assistant usually has carefully defined areas of responsibility and may be shielded from those managerial tasks. You may love the assistant, who is the bright and shining star always doing things that make you smile. But it may well be that the assistant does not have the right gifts for leading the parish into the next chapter of its story, or that the assistant has a different view of what should happen next. If you want the assistant because you think she will keep things exactly as they are, you may be surprised. If you want the assistant because you think he will be as warm and ingratiating a rector as he was an assistant, you may be surprised. Your assumptions on how the assistant would function as rector are exactly that: assumptions. And before you reach for what feels like a comforting or quick solution for the uneasy state of transition, know that hard experience throughout the Episcopal Church has shown us that it is unlikely that such a transition is wise.

VI

Particular Considerations for Challenged Parishes and for Challenging Times

Challenged Parishes: Growing Smaller and Poorer

At a recent gathering of a group of transition ministers, the conversation turned to the large number of parishes that can no longer afford a solo full-time priest. The numbers told the story: thirty-two dioceses had sent their transition ministers, among them they had sixty-four open positions for full-time clergy, they had three hundred seventeen positions for part-time clergy, and they had fifty-seven clergy who had asked to be presented to the group as seeking a new call. In the past, there were more priests seeking new calls, there were ample full-time calls to consider and discern, and part-time positions were not shared for consideration.

This phenomenon is not exclusive to these dioceses; it is true nationally, both in the Episcopal Church and in other denominations. It requires creativity, honesty, and flexibility on the part of all the stakeholders.

When the rector has told the vestry they are departing, the vestry will want to check with the diocesan transition ministry officer to determine what the compensation guidelines are for priests in the diocese, and if there are any particular market forces at play locally. For example, parishes located in an area with a high cost of living may struggle to meet the compensation requirements of a priest if there is no rectory to offer. Rural parishes may struggle to attract priests, since many—but not all—of the younger and newly ordained priests seem to prefer calls in urban settings. Getting the basics like diocesan compensation minimums will give the vestry a sense of whether they can afford a full-time priest, particularly given the cost of health insurance. Vestries need to know very early in the process what they can afford in terms of compensation and what options are available to them. It may also be helpful to review what the average compensation looks like for parishes in your part of the diocese and of your size.

Options vary: you may want to consider sharing a priest with another small parish. This is not quite the same as yoking: the two parishes continue with their own lay leadership and distinct identities; they simply come to an agreement to share ordained leadership. This requires great clarity in the agreement between the two parishes as to expectations. Sometimes there is fear related to access to the priest in case of emergency. In many parishes, though, a solo priest is attending to emergent pastoral needs for several parishioners at the same time. Any of those parishioners might worry about access to the priest, though they usually do not. If a parish that is sharing feels that it is competing for the priest's time and attention, however, particularly if the priest has been working with one parish for a long time and this agreement has been a "marriage of convenience" for financial purposes, there needs to be a deep conversation that will help ease those fears.

Another frequently heard objection to a sharing scheme is that the priest might not be one whom they would choose—"How could a priest be right both for Saint Swithen's and us? We're two entirely different kinds of people!" In reality, unless the two congregations are wildly different in liturgical practice or in theological bent, many priests could effectively serve both.

This configuration would most likely require some shifting in service times, and perhaps the shrinking of number of services. Oftentimes the "8 o'clockers" are passionate about going to that service at that time. Their numbers may have dwindled to four people on most Sundays, and yet they are adamant that the service must remain. Similarly, two parishes that both have services at 10 a.m. are going to have to come to an agreement as to how the times are going to shift. Ideally, both will shift their times, because there will be much grief if one congregation gets to retain its service time and the other has to cede that time. One pair of parishes that shares a priest opted to have two services per month at one parish and two (plus fifth Sundays) at the other. This has not been ideal, since it has proven confusing for newcomers and for some of the elderly members, but it is the choice that currently feels right for these two churches.

Some dioceses formally yoke small congregations; it is the wisdom of the diocesan leadership that guides such decisions. In such a case, if new ordained leadership is required for the new entity, there is a single vestry which proceeds in the same manner as any other full-time call. The only caveat would be that if this is a new pairing, particular care should be taken that both of the original congregations feel their voices have been fully heard and their hopes and dreams for the yoked faith community will be considered. In one parish consisting of two congregations, yoked for many years, one congregation (historically African American and smaller than the other) felt they had been treated as unequal partners for much of the history of the yoking. When it was time for a new priest to be called, the interim rector led focused work on their history to lay bare the stories of pain versus privilege, and the lay leadership was intentional in the naming of a discernment committee with equal representation from both congregations. For this parish, the transition time was one of truth-telling and healing. Their call did not end the continued deepening of relationship and transformative work of the Holy Spirit.

Another option some dioceses are considering, but which requires deep discernment and preparation, is actually a very ancient one: having lay or diaconal pastoral leaders who carry out much of the work of ministry, utilizing "circuit rider" priests who offer those sacraments that cannot otherwise be administered. This reflects back to the early days of the Episcopal Church in the United States, particularly in the southern states. In a sense, this is what the apostle Paul did in his missionary travels, before there was an infrastructure of church with canons and constitutions. Local formation programs for ordination and lay leadership (Iona School,[1] Bishop Kemper School)[2] as well as creative partnering of laity and clergy such as the Total

---

1. *http://www.ionaschool.com/.*

2. *https://www.bishopkemperschool.org/.*

Ministry program begun twenty years ago in the Diocese of Michigan are a response to the need for creativity and flexibility.

There is, however, a need to look at the hardest situation: a church that is no longer sustainable. Perhaps it is a rural parish with no endowment, no increase in population in the area, and no prospects for growth. Perhaps it is a church with little in the way of resources and in geographic proximity to a larger church with more to attract new parishioners. Perhaps it is a church in a community where the population around it has changed dramatically, and there is neither the will on the part of the parish nor the desire on the part of the community to reimagine ministry.

This is the painful truth: like human beings, churches have a lifespan. Some lifespans are longer than others. Sometimes the greatest gift is to permit the small group of the faithful who remain and who are tired to complete their ministry with grace and thanksgiving, respecting the needs—and grief—of parishioners as they prepare for the church to close its doors. This may require a period of discernment, with a priest who can serve as a spiritual guide and comforter as well as a teller of the truth in love. One parish went through a yearlong process of such discernment. They had little money left in their coffers, and it was important to them that those resources be given to charities in their small community that could serve the hungry. They loved each other, they loved their shared history, but they were cognizant that their situation was dire and that a restart or re-visioning process would not save them. So they said thanks be to God, had a meaningful rite of leave-taking, and found other church homes. Perhaps the physical reminder of their history—the church building—was no longer there for them, but this was more than offset by the memories of what they had in the past and the vibrant new relationships they were forming as they found their new church homes, even the most senior among them.

Another church, a historically African American church that had dwindled to a half dozen parishioners, closed their doors after several months of discernment. Most of the members then worshiped in the nearby Euro American Episcopal church where in prior decades they had not been welcomed. Both congregations knew their history, wanted to create a new story together, and with the guidance of the priest-in-charge, found a way to build that story.

In contrast, another historically African American congregation was determined to retain their unique identity and personality. This church was attended by what was essentially a large extended family group. They understood their finances, even with supplementation by their diocese, could not support a full-time priest. They secured a part-time priest who understood their particular needs. This was a stopgap measure, not a solution, but it was sufficient for that faith community at the time. They know it will be a continuing challenge in the years to come.

Some dioceses are more proactive than others in guiding churches with these kinds of challenges. Some regularly do yoking or similar clustering of ministry to keep parishes going. Each parish and each diocese is different. If this is the situation your parish faces, have a frank conversation with your bishop and the diocesan team to see what the practices are in your context and how best to proceed.

Calling a priest in hope that the new priest will be the savior, causing new members to flock through the doors is wishful thinking, and a recipe for disappointment and resentment. Clarity about what can and should be done, and about what gifts might help, is critically important, and can help shape your decision about seeking a new ordained leader in challenging circumstances. Consult with your bishop to determine what makes best sense for your parish.

Challenged Parishes: Bad/Sad/Mad Endings

On occasion, the departure of a priest may be the result of conflict or of a decline in energy in their ministry, or may be because there was misconduct. This is always a source of pain for all involved and does impact the transition process.

Conflict may be a long-standing pattern in this congregation or may have been specific to a particular event or a particular situation. Often, dioceses offer consultants to work with such a congregation to try and resolve matters informally. Sometimes this resolves the conflict; other times it yields a formal dissolution of the relationship between the priest and the congregation, as outlined in Title III.9.15 of the Constitution and Canons of the Episcopal Church.[3] On occasion it is handled more informally and the relationship simply ends by mutual agreement.

Priests may lose their effectiveness as leaders. The parish membership or the community may have changed, the things that worked before are not working anymore, or there may be particularly determined lay leaders who feel a change is called for. The priest may decide that it is time for departure, or may feel backed into a corner and so decides to depart.

On rare occasions, clergy misconduct may require that the priest leave. Generally, such changes are the result of a formal disciplinary process (Title IV in the Constitution and Canons of the Episcopal Church)[4] and the priest may be required to take administrative leave, departing the congregation before the Title IV process is completed. Alternatively, the priest may be required to depart after the process is completed and a finding is made. This process takes time, tries to approach the hard work in as pastoral way as possible, and invariably causes grief and stress in the congregation.

In each of these endings, there is work that needs to be done prior to getting into the work of the transition process. This is a case where the right intentional interim and the right team of helpers in the work can make all the difference.

In all these types of situations, there will be residual anger and grief. If there was conflict between the priest and the lay leaders or the congregation as a whole, it may feel like there was never a resolution of that conflict. The priest left. While some might have felt relief, others might have appreciated the priest's ministry and the latter group don't understand what happened, or think that the ones who didn't appreciate the priest are to blame. If there was a pattern of conflict in the congregation, there might be a deep-seated distrust of ordained leadership and/or the diocese that is reinforced by the present circumstances. Those who wanted the priest gone might have thought "this time it will be different," but then the pattern reasserted itself

---

3. Currently available as a download here: *https://www.generalconvention.org/publications#CandC*.

4. For a detailed explanation of this process, see *www.titleiv.org*.

and it played out just as it had before. The conflict might have been based on a different style of leadership than that of a beloved prior rector, even though the new priest was called specifically for a different set of gifts.

All of these situations call for some prayerful and professional guidance before moving into the actual work of transition. Remember that one of the first stages of this work is that of self-study. If parishioners are angry, tired, sad, or confused, the data that is gathered will be skewed and the results will be unhelpful. Addressing these issues first gives the discernment committee a much better chance to hear what the congregation hopes for in the future, rather than speaking from a place of reactivity. It's worthwhile mentioning that even in the most graceful of departures (the completion of a long and effective tenure by the departing rector, the election of the rector to the episcopate, a long-awaited and well-earned retirement), there is an element of grief and loss. This is why it is recommended that there be a fallow period before appointing a discernment committee; parishioners need some time to work through those feelings, and they need some time to imagine their parish with someone new at the helm. Otherwise the tendency may be to try and find someone identical to the priest who just left, who was just right for that season of ministry but might not be the perfect model of what they need for the coming season.

This is also why this work of healing needs to be done *before* the process begins when the departure was under unhappy circumstances. As humans, we tend to have to sort out what just happened, and it takes a while (and sometimes some professional guidance by a trained consultant in partnership with the intentional interim) to achieve sufficient perspective to be able to imagine what a happy future might look like—God's vision for the parish—after suffering a painful time. Your bishop and your TMO will be good sources for consultants, or for whatever support they deem necessary before you start your transition process.

It is true, though, that there will be parishioners who want to "put the past behind us" or "get on with it" in hopes that the new priest will solve all problems. Invariably, these are the same parishioners who don't want any mention of "the recent unpleasantness" in the community ministry portfolio. This loops back to comments made elsewhere in this book about being honest with potential candidates. It greatly increases the risk that the incoming priest will have an unhappy tenure if they are either expected to do all the healing work before they even know the parishioners or don't know what emotional waters they are entering.[5] In some ways, this preparatory healing work is akin to going from the hospital after surgery to a rehab facility, where those with special skills prepare the patient to be able to go home safely and well.

Challenging Times

As this is being written, the nation is in the grip of a pandemic, COVID-19. It has changed the way we function as church; it has created a dramatic change in the financial condition of many congregations; and it has caused congregations in transition to wonder how to do the work of transition under these conditions.

Challenging times are nothing new. Parishes who were in transition when a massive hurricane or tornado hit their community, when the bottom fell out of the nation's economy, when a national tragedy such as 9/11 occurred or we faced the onset of war, all wrestled with whether or not to proceed, whether or not there could be a God-centered and faithful process, whether or not they could afford to dream and hope about the future.

Every congregation's situation has its own particularities, and every diocese may view the appropriate strategy a little differently. Your bishop and your transition minister are your starting points to determine the diocese's view on things.

There are some considerations that you might reflect upon as you decide what is right for your church.

---

5. A classic story about such a situation: a priest had conflict with his lay leadership because of his relationship activities in the wake of his divorce. The priest departed under great pressure from the lay leadership. Although the bishop knew the circumstances, this information was not conveyed to the newly called priest who followed. For a year, the new priest would get signals of distrust from some parishioners, who would never say why, or would get odd responses when speaking of the appropriate pastoral response to those whose marriages were ending. It took a year of trust-building and patience to finally learn the story. The priest was able to reshape her ministry to be responsive to these sore spots, and did some intensive work with those who were most emotionally enmeshed in the bad situation to help them to heal, but it meant that other work that she had been called to do had to be put on a back burner for several months.

First, give yourself the time and space to make major decisions if a major event has occurred, such as a natural disaster, an economic crisis, or a pandemic. Clergy and pastoral care providers often tell those who have suffered the death of a spouse that they should wait at least a year before selling the house, or moving to Oklahoma, or remarrying. While we wouldn't give a timeframe as fixed as a year, we would say that making a big decision about an element of your transition while emotions are very high may not be wise.

Here's a story of two congregations in the midst of the COVID-19 pandemic: one was about halfway through their transition process when the pandemic hit. This parish was a healthy midsized congregation, with people who remembered past transitions as ones that yielded wonderful calls. "The Lord has taken us through this process before, and we have no doubt he will take us through this one now, and it will all be good" were the words of one former warden. The vestry assumed its proper role of leadership during the transition and was realistic about the parish's strengths and challenges. The self-study process was clear and honest, with results shared with the parish as a whole. The pandemic hit just as they were completing their community ministry portfolio. They had noted a small downturn in their giving, even though they were offering online giving, but had experienced lively participation in virtual worship services. In fact, the numbers for online attendance were significantly higher than prior to the pandemic. They felt confident that they would be able to offer a competitive compensation package, even though they didn't have much in the way of endowment funds, because this was a place with a history of giving, and giving well. This pandemic was, in their eyes, a temporary issue that had created new opportunities for evangelism and missional work, and they knew that would not fade after the pandemic was over. They had learned new things, and were delighted. They proceeded with their search and made a wise and healthy call.

In contrast, another church struggled. This was a place that had experienced conflict in the past and had traditionally been somewhat isolated. Nevertheless, the process went reasonably well, although there were some tensions on occasion between the discernment committee and the vestry. The CMP was published, and they received several candidates. The final recommendation appeared to be a strong candidate, with many of the qualities the parish sought. Still, when the vestry met the candidate (virtually, since by this time the pandemic had shut down the possibility of visiting the candidate in their parish or bringing the candidate to the calling parish), some had a sense that this was not the right fit. Even though they were advised that they shouldn't proceed if they had a sense that the call wasn't of the Holy Spirit, they felt parishioners would be angry if they "had someone and let them slip away." Everyone felt uncomfortable.

These two stories highlight some key factors in how and if a parish may proceed with a transition process in challenging times:

1. What is the congregation's sense of God's providence? Do they trust that the Holy Spirit will give them the wisdom to make faithful choices? A key indicator is the parish's prayer life: do they revert to secular language when difficult things happen or do they stop and pray? Do they remember that asking God for help is the starting place in difficult times? If their hearts are not God-centered, their anxiety will win out over their listening for God's voice and over plain common sense.

2. What is the congregation's level of financial stability? If they are on very shaky ground and believe that there will be a "magic priest" who will solve all their problems, their anxiety will cloud their understanding of their capacity. Their responses to the questions in the CMP will be forward-looking in the wrong way: when they are asked how they operate (a key framing of questions in the narrative section of the CMP), they will respond with how they hope they will operate in the future, painting an inaccurate picture of what the priest would encounter if called.

3. What is the congregation's sense of unity, mutual appreciation, and support? If they are locking arms to do the work to seek God's will for their parish, this will help them weather the uncertainties of a call in difficult times. It will also be evident in the information gathered in the self-study activities and the discernment committee's responses to the questions in the CMP. It will also shape the demeanor of the discernment committee and the vestry when they interview candidates. If, however, this is an anxious community with a prior history of conflict, there may be too much anxiety to yield valid data, too much of a desire

to present a rosy picture when filling out the CMP, and too much worry about funds to make an honest commitment in a letter of agreement.

What to do in a situation like this? Proceeding with a process may be unwise, both for the parish and any priest who is considering the call. Your bishop and their leadership team may advise you to accept an assigned priest-in-charge for a fixed period of time, to help you weather the crisis and reassess after some semblance of normalcy has returned. Alternatively, in some dioceses, an interim may be appointed but the start of the actual search activities will be delayed. Yet another model is for someone to serve as a part-time "supply plus pastoral care" priest to cover sacramental and pastoral needs during the crisis. All of these options have pros and cons, but proceeding with a transition process in the midst of a crisis when there are too many issues that could get in the way of listening for the wisdom of the Holy Spirit has the potential to compound an already difficult situation. Go slow and make wise choices; Jesus Christ is walking with you in this, just as he did accompanying the two disheartened disciples walking to Emmaus.

VII

FOR THE DISCERNMENT COMMITTEE: PHASE ONE

Congratulations! You have been invited by your vestry to serve on the discernment committee (sometimes called the search committee).

What is your role, what is your work, and how do you do this holy work?

In this chapter, we will lay out the first half of the process that you will follow. Some decisions have already been made by the vestry,[1] but there will be ample opportunities for you as a committee to decide the best way to use the tools contained here for your parish. We know that you know the parish better than we diocesan staff do, and this process respects that reality.

First things first: you are a community whose work must be centered in prayer. The nature of calling a priest is not like a secular hiring process: it is about entering into a covenantal relationship with someone who will be a part of your spiritual journey.

So if it has not yet been done by the vestry or some other group, you should devise a prayer for the search process. This prayer should be prayed at every worship service, at every meeting, in your own prayer lives. In other words, it should become the embodiment of the parish's transition, your request that God guide you and give you grace.

Many committees have found it helpful to do a study on the call of David and his anointing by Samuel to be king of Israel (1 Sam. 16:1–13).

---

1. If you want to take a deep dive into those decisions and how they made them, take a look at the chapter entitled "For the Vestry: Phase One."

It is a way to frame the work that you will do to seek a priest with the right gifts and graces for the parish in the years to come.

Blessings as you do this important work, but remember: you do not do it alone. Those on your bishop's staff who assist in the transition process are there to help you, and you have your bishop's support as chief pastor of the diocese.

An Overview of the Work Ahead

Your diocese takes seriously the challenges and joys inherent in transition. Whether your priest is retiring or taking another call, this "in-between time" can be an opportunity for accepting the loss of a beloved pastor, for healing old wounds, for discovering how the church and its surrounding community has changed since the last call, and for imagining how God is calling the church to be the body of Christ now and in the future. There will be anxiety about this future, but, approached faithfully, there may also be great discovery and growth.

Each church is unique, so each search is unique. However, there are certain principles that guide all churches during transition.

It is likely that your priest has already left by the time you read this, since discernment committees are usually formed after the incumbent's departure. There may be a tendency to want to reach back to ask questions of your trusted spiritual guide, but this is a time to practice letting go and looking forward.

Now is the time to prepare for the future. If there are old wounds, work is necessary to move toward identification and healing. If there are process or systems issues that need attention—and every church has some—work is necessary to identify and modify them.

Your task as a discernment committee is to help the parish do a self-study based on three questions:

- Who have we been?
- Who are we now?
- Who is God calling us to be?

Here is another way to think of your work:

You Will Build a Map of the Past, Present, and Future

Discern where the parish has been, where it is today, and where God is calling it to be in the future.

See what kinds of gifts and graces are already present in the parish that can move it to where God is calling it to be.

Identify those gifts and skills you'll need in your next priest, augmenting what you've already got, to assist you in that process.

This kind of self-study is practical, information-gathering work; it is also spiritual discernment work, listening for God's voice. Some dioceses offer consultants to assist you; you may choose to do it all without a consultant. Many parishes do.

You Will Draw the Map for Candidates to Understand Where Your Future Lies

You will build a body of information that identifies the gifts and graces you need from your next priest, based upon what you've discovered, what your dreams, hopes, and aspirations are for your parish, and what the challenges ahead may be. This will feed the community ministry portfolio (more on that later), which will be posted on the Episcopal Church database[2] and will be accessed by potential candidates. This document, partnered with your website, will invite candidates into conversation with you as you mutually discern if there is a fit.[3]

You Will Choose Your Guide

Assess the applications of those who seek to serve as your next priest. You want to see if the gifts and graces they offer match your needs. You also

---

2. *www.otmportfolio.org.*

3. In the past, parishes published profiles that described their church, their community, their programs, and what they were seeking in their next priest. They were hard work for the committee—is there anything quite so painful as writing by committee?—and added months on to the process. They were essentially marketing brochures for the position being offered and, frankly, were not terribly helpful for priests to discern whether the parish was a fit for their gifts or not. Many dioceses have gotten away from such an approach, since the vast majority of the information that was in the old profiles is now, or should be, on the parish's website. The small portion of information that would not be on your website is on the community ministry portfolio that you will fill out to promote your position, and that document also contains a series of questions that help illustrate how you operate as a faith community in ways that are much more helpful to priest candidates.

want to see who has the right "chemistry" to do well in your parish, to get you to where God is leading you next. You will seek "the One": the person to whom the Holy Spirit has led you. The discernment committee will recommend this candidate to the vestry, who will meet with the person, and their spouse if applicable, and will vote on whether this is your next priest. Your bishop and the bishop's staff will have a part in this as well, assisting in the vetting process and giving final approval of the call.

Your tasks are quite specific. You will study the parish, with input from the congregation. You will publish a vestry- and bishop-approved community ministry portfolio, which provides an overview of the church and its vision.

You may advise your parish, if necessary, to improve its website, which will include relevant and up-to-date information on the church and the search process, for the benefit of both potential candidates and potential parishioners.

Once the community ministry portfolio is published, along with whatever other mechanisms you use to publicize your call with the advice of your diocesan transition ministry officer, you will receive names, interview candidates, visit a short list of candidates in their own ministry setting, and select a single finalist[4] to recommend to your vestry after all necessary vetting is completed. This includes a formal background check, a call from the bishop to the candidate's bishop if the candidate is from outside the diocese, and a call or visit between the bishop and the candidate.

The vestry will meet the recommended candidate and will then vote on the finalist you've recommended. Once your recommendation is affirmed, the vestry extends a call. If the call is accepted, the vestry and the candidate negotiate a letter of agreement. Your work is essentially done at this point, but you may not be discharged from your duties until the candidate, the senior warden, and the bishop sign the letter of agreement.

---

4. It is the practice of some dioceses to permit the vestry to ask for multiple names. This seems to fly in the face of the delegation of responsibility from the vestry to the discernment committee. It also creates the possibility that the vestry will replicate the work the committee has already done, and may not have the time or energy to discern as deeply as the discernment committee has done. We recommend against this practice, but understand that contexts may differ.

Communications and Vestry/Committee Interaction during the Time of Transition

There should be regular "check-in" meetings between the wardens and the chair(s) of the discernment committee, focused primarily on progress in the steps of transition. It's also a good idea to have periodic meetings of the chair(s) and the whole vestry, particularly if the process is leading to work that requires participation of the whole congregation (surveys, focus groups, "town hall meetings"). This is useful because it is an opportunity to flag communication needs, resource needs, or rough spots that would benefit from the wisdom of the vestry. It also provides the opportunity to make presentations about progress, such as survey or focus group results and draft responses to the narrative questions in the community ministry portfolio.

Some discernment committees run their survey questions by the vestry if there might be challenging questions to ask. The purpose of this is not to have the vestry micromanage your questions so much as it is to help the vestry to field any questions or negative feedback about a particular question.

The vestry will need to provide some data to the discernment committee, such as what the compensation package for the next priest will look like. The vestry will also need to review and approve the content of the community ministry portfolio prior to its publication.

"Where we are in the process" updates, either published in the parish newsletter or bulletin, or presented during announcement time during services, remind parishioners that things are happening even if those things aren't visible to them.

It is a useful thing for the discernment committee to present an adult forum talking about what has been published to promote the position in the community ministry portfolio. Generally, we recommend that this revolve around the answers to the narrative questions rather than the nuts and bolts of the numbers. This should be viewed as a sharing of information, not an opportunity for group editing of what has already been published.

It's important to share enough information that everyone has a sense of forward motion in the process, but there is some information that requires COMPLETE CONFIDENTIALITY.

When you start to receive applications from prospective candidates, you can say nothing about candidates. Not the number of applications, not whether Father Fred applied, not whether there are any women candidates, not where applicants come from. Nothing, not even to your nearest and dearest.

Your response to any inquiry about these things is something along the lines of "we are not allowed to share any of those details, and I'm sure you wouldn't want me to compromise the process by sharing confidential information. Please keep us in prayer as we discern God's will for our beloved parish."

One more thing: often parishioners will approach you with ideas for candidates. Because we want a level playing field for all candidates, here's a graceful way to handle it: say "Thank you so much for telling me about Father Fred. Once our parish's community ministry portfolio is up on the national database, please do encourage Father Fred to review it and decide whether or not he feels called to discern with us. We'll let everyone know when it's posted!" In other words, the burden is on the parishioner to reach out to Father Fred, not on the discernment committee. Then the burden is on the priest to discern whether or not they wish to apply. Frequently, such priests have no interest in making a move at this time, and it is their decision whether or not they want to apply. If that parishioner asks if Father Fred applied, you can say "all those who discerned they wanted to apply have applied, and I'm afraid I am not permitted to tell you whether or not he is among them. But we know that the Holy Spirit will guide us all, both the candidates and the discernment committee, as we work together to fulfill God's will."

Lastly, many parishes choose to have a page on their website relating to the search process. It usually does not contain a link to your parish's community ministry portfolio on the database, since all priests know where to find that. It might, however, point to information about the community, updates on the search process, and other such information. This is yet another place where your prayer for discernment might be published.

The Self-Study Process

Remember those three questions that will inform your understanding of what the parish might need? You'll need tools to get at the answers, and this book contains a toolkit for you. There are a variety of ways you can find those answers, but which tools you might pick to get them will vary from parish to parish. What works in a little parish with fewer than fifty active members is very different from a parish with over five hundred active members. So as you look into the toolkit that follows, imagine using each of these tools in your setting. Some will give you data to answer more than one of those three questions. *You do not need to use all of these tools, just what you need to get the data you seek. Spend more time on the present than the past, and spend more time on the future (the hard work of discernment) than the present.*

Your goal in the first half of the process (all of which is addressed in this chapter) is to prepare the community ministry portfolio, the primary document that will help potential candidates understand who you are as a parish, and what gifts and graces you seek in your next priest to help you live into God's will for the parish in the next chapter of its story.

Tools for Self-Study

Question One: "Who Have We Been?"

We begin the self-study by examining our history as a parish. Often, there are parish histories that have been written at important anniversaries. These are a great starting point. They give us much information about when things happened and who was involved. However, because they were written at a time of celebration, they rarely tell the whole story.

Moments of struggle, of conflict, of disappointment, or of shame are usually not included. Despite the negative tone, they are as important, if not more important, than the stories of glory and triumph. We cannot see the beauty of the light unless we also show the shadows. This is why in the Psalms we hear the stories of loss and despair as well as the songs of praise—all of this is part of the human condition, and it shapes us. We need to tell the whole story, not just the shiny parts.

So how do we get the rest of the story?

One place we can turn is to the social science of ethnography, the systematic study of people and their cultures. In the parish setting, this means looking at a particular faith family, their story, how they interact, what their values are, what their culture has been and is.

Congregational Timeline

A particularly powerful ethnographic tool for learning the parish's history is the congregational timeline.[5] This is a group activity for all generations. The parishioners gather in a large room, sometimes in a social setting such as a potluck dinner, and start mapping out their understanding of the parish's story. The parish's story is tied to individual stories, to the changes in the parish physical plant, to clergy leadership, and to the larger world. Check out the description of how to conduct one of these exercises in the relevant footnote below. One of the most interesting things that will appear is patterns. When did the greatest growth periods occur in the parish? Was it related to a particular priest, or was it when the new elementary school was built nearby? Was there a pattern around building projects? Did the priest usually leave after each building project (not an uncommon occurrence)? Many of the times of change have both good and less-than-good things associated with them, and we can discover things that are important to know. Because it works best when the majority of parishioners participate, this works better for smaller congregations than larger ones.

Interviewing the Elders

When Mary and Joseph came to the temple with the infant Jesus for his presentation, the first people who clearly understood who this child was were the two elders, Anna and Simeon. Their lives of faithful service and worship at the temple gave them insights. Their length of life gave them experience and perspective. These elders brought a message of incredible importance . . . and elders in our parishes can do the same.

Thus, another tool for studying the history of a congregation is interviewing elders, those parishioners who have been members for many years,

---

5. *See https://studyingcongregations.org/thinking-about-congregations/methods-of-understanding/congregational-time-line/.* This website provides a great description of the congregational timeline exercise, as well as many other excellent tools for congregational study.

or even for their whole lives. The approach that is recommended is called the semistructured interview. The interviewer begins with a series of pre-planned questions, but also includes some questions that invite more open-ended responses, should the interview provide the opportunity to explore some interesting details. Some interviewers record these interviews on their cellphone or on a digital recorder, although some interviewees find recordings off-putting. After the interview, notes should be written up. After all of the interviews are completed, a team should review and compare the notes for themes and repeated stories.

Archaeology

It's time for a dig! Most parishes have extensive minutes of vestry meetings, as well as documentation of important changes such as letters of agreement with new clergy, approval for a mortgage for a new building, and such.

Have someone who loves to research take a look at those documents. Were there surprises? Battles? There often are at changes of clergy and at times of building projects. Are there questions that are raised by terms of letters of agreement? Sometimes a clause is inserted into such an agreement after something troubling happened with the prior incumbent.[6]

There's also a certain amount of archaeology associated with the physical plant, its décor, liturgical fittings, and such. The architecture tells a story: many churches built in the mid-1950s were in the Scandinavian style, midcentury modern. Was that the style of the neighborhood? Was another church of another denomination built in the area around the same time? Perhaps the architect gave the church a discount to replicate large portions of the design. Are the altar hangings and other décor designed in a more traditional style? Did they come from another building or parish, or was this a nod to an altar guild that wanted a more old-fashioned style? Keep your eyes open for oddities. There is always a story behind the oddity.

---

6. An example: a priest lived in the rectory for several years with two very large and not-well-trained dogs. There had been no regular check of the condition of the rectory, so when the priest retired, it was discovered that woodwork had been chewed on and the basement smelled of dog urine and excrement. It was expensive to remediate this problem, and it was difficult but necessary for this small parish to address the issue before their new priest arrived. The letter of agreement for the new priest required annual walk-throughs to note any issues with the rectory that needed to be addressed. This is a wise practice in any LOA when a rectory is involved, but understanding the backstory would explain some tense conversations with candidates for their next priest about pets!

In one parish, the campus was set into a rolling plot of land back a couple of hundred yards from the main road. There was a beautiful carved wooden sign at the entrance. There was lovely landscaping around the buildings, and a beautiful woodland glade where the memorial garden was set. There were also some ugly tree stumps. What was the story? Originally, the church buildings were invisible from the road because of the heavily wooded land facing the road. The parish received a diocesan grant to fund the removal of many of the trees and to get the new sign, but there were no funds left to grind out the stumps. In later years, several people raised the issue of the unattractive stumps, but it never was a high enough priority to set aside funds to attend to it.

In another parish, the church was similarly built into a heavily wooded property, but the trees were never cut down. The founding priest, a contemplative, envisioned the church as a sanctuary, sheltered from the noise and chaos of the world. The church was invisible to drivers on the road nearby, and that was the way the founding priest liked it. It became part of the culture of the place that it was a hermitage of sorts, and the only growth it experienced was word-of-mouth conversations between members and those who were their friends. As the church membership dwindled two priests later, bringing up the removal of some of the trees so the church would be more visible caused great consternation. No one remembered the original reason why there was no desire to make the church structure visible from the road, but there was some shared feeling that it would change the essential nature of the congregation, and people fought that possibility without knowing why.

What else do you see? A tired felt banner that is faded may be a sign of a precious relationship or a lack of energy for someone to replace it, or both. When, if ever, was the building modified and why? Might it have been for growth, for accessibility, or for adding ministries? Perhaps it might be related to a particular project now no longer in existence. Did the champion of the project leave, and if so, why? This sort of exploration may reveal patterns of conflict.

What is in the literal and figurative closets? In one parish, there are sets of tablecloths in two closets in the parish hall, one for fellowship and one for a particular fundraising group. What was the story? At one point, the leaders of the two groups did not get along, and each purchased enough tablecloths for their events. Over time, the persons involved passed away or left, and no one knew the original story, but the pattern of the two sets of tablecloths remained. Many parishes have similar stories.

Look at pictures on the walls, especially those of cherished lay leaders. This can give you clues as to those values or characteristics that are lifted up in the congregation.

You might also look at the length of tenure of prior incumbents. Often there are a series of photographs or portraits of past priests, with the dates beneath. Were their departures happy or sad?

As always, look for patterns of behavior, examples of values that have been cherished across generations, and how the parish behaves under stress.

Question Two: Who We Are Now, by the Numbers?

One of the ways we tell the story of our parish is by looking at numbers. If you've ever seen the annual parochial report each parish is required to provide the diocese (and the national church), it's all about the numbers.

On your parochial report, some of the key numbers that are tracked are these:

1. Average Sunday attendance vs. numbers of parishioners on the parish rolls.
2. Total dollar amounts of pledges and loose-plate giving each year.
3. Total operating budget each year.

Numbers are a very "blunt object" way of seeing what's happening in a parish, and *they are not the whole story, but they can lead us to ask questions about the rest of the story*, and they are very important when we write a description of the parish.

Where do you get this information? As I said, it's on your parochial report, and that should be part of the vestry minutes.

The Episcopal Church website can give you some of this data, since it is reported in your annual parochial report. You'll find a trove of material in the "Research and Statistics" section of that website, at *https://www.*

episcopalchurch.org/research-and-statistics. Scroll down. This will bring you to the option to "Parochial Report—Explore Trends," and clicking on it will allow you to find your parish in your diocese. You can look at several different data points for a ten-year period (I've used St. Matthew's in Sterling, Virginia, as an example). There's an overview page.

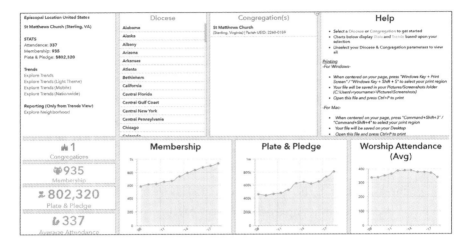

You can see a variety of information on this page, and you can also click for a closer view of key markers, like Giving Trends, Membership, and Average Sunday Attendance:

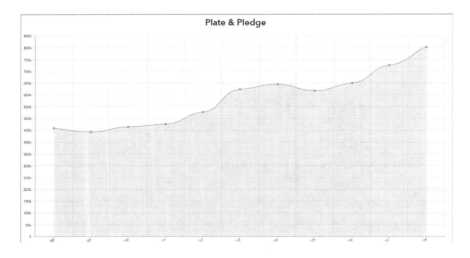

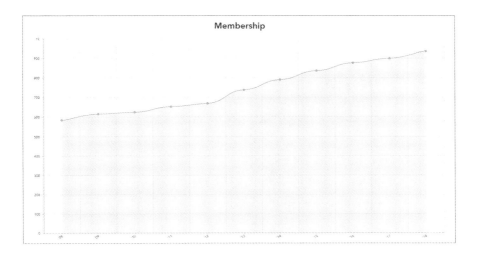

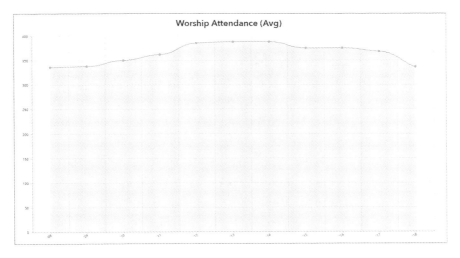

Their membership chart tells us that they've got 935 people on the parish rolls. Their ASA chart tells us that they have an average Sunday attendance (ASA) of almost 340. Their plate and pledge chart tells us that combined pledge and plate income is just over $800,000. The trends are upward for all categories except for ASA, but that is not entirely surprising. Among newer members, particularly among new members who are younger families (a category that is growing for them), patterns of Sunday attendance are often less than every Sunday.

You might also look at your own parish's full parochial report, which your vestry can give you, to see how average pledge and numbers of pledging units have changed over the past five years or so. It's great if the total pledge dollars have increased, but these two other data points tell you if a few people are giving more, if more people are giving who didn't give before, and whether the pledges are reacting to economic conditions. Simply divide the total pledge amount from the parochial report by the number of pledging units to get the figure for each year.

You could also use other resources or basic census data to get a closer look at the economic conditions of your area. The Episcopal Church now offers a rich variety of demographic information through an interactive report called the "Know Your Neighbood" Report. The very same place where parochial report statistics were found in the past will give you this information with a click on "Know Your Neighborhood." Let's see how the data looks in St. Matthew's case.

Remember that website that gave you the charts above? Click on "Explore Neighborhood" for a variety of interesting demographic and financial data about the community within a five-mile radius of the building. The radius can be adjusted to a one-mile radius, a five-mile radius, and a ten-mile radius.

This allows for a view of population growth projected for the area (in this case, it is projected to grow 1.31 percent, which sounds small, but given the population density, it's significant) and if there is a particular age pattern to the growth (it's pretty stable, with an average age in the mid-30s) or ethnic change to the growth (it's a majority Caucasian demographic, with growth among Asian Americans and Hispanic/Latinx persons). Education level is high. While the images for this report look static, in a real report, there are drop-down menus that give much more detail.

Median household income (as opposed to disposable income) in that county is $136,000—one of the wealthiest counties in the nation. Let's take a look at the average pledge in 2018. Divide the $570,000 in dollars pledged by 107 pledges,[7] for an average pledge of $5,327.

---

7. Of the over $802,000 in plate and pledge receipts, the pledge dollars were $570,000, per the detailed information on their parochial report.

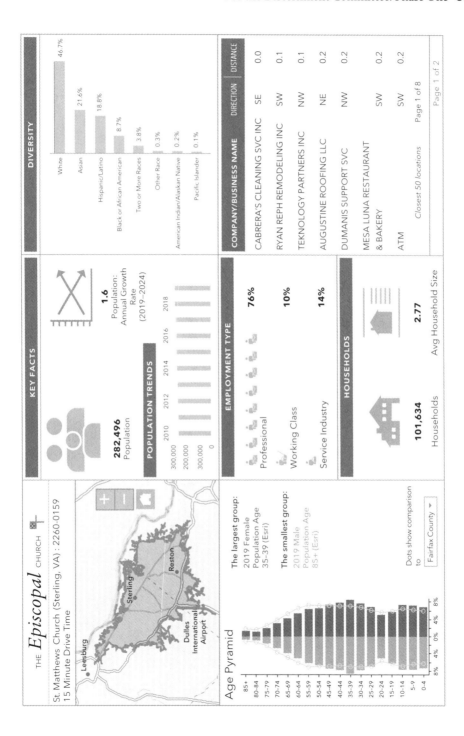

THE *Episcopal* CHURCH

St. Matthews Church (Sterling, VA) : 2260-0159
15 Minute Drive Time

Leesburg
Sterling
Reston
Dulles International Airport

Age Pyramid

The largest group:
2019 Female Population Age 35-39 (Esri)

The smallest group:
2019 Male Population Age 85+ (Esri)

Dots show comparison to
Fairfax County ▸

85+
80-84
75-79
70-74
65-69
60-64
55-59
50-54
45-49
40-44
35-39
30-34
25-29
20-24
15-19
10-14
5-9
0-4

8% 4% 0% 4% 8%

KEY FACTS

282,496
Population

1.6
Population: Annual Growth Rate (2019–2024)

POPULATION TRENDS

300,000
200,000
300,000
0

2010 2012 2014 2016 2018

EMPLOYMENT TYPE

76%
Professional

10%
Working Class

14%
Service Industry

HOUSEHOLDS

101,634
Households

2.77
Avg Household Size

DIVERSITY

White — 46.7%
Asian — 21.6%
Hispanic/Latino — 18.8%
Black or African American — 8.7%
Two or More Races — 3.8%
Other Race — 0.3%
American Indian/Alaskan Native — 0.2%
Pacific Islander — 0.1%

COMPANY/BUSINESS NAME	DIRECTION	DISTANCE
CABRERA'S CLEANING SVC INC	SE	0.0
RYAN REPH REMODELING INC	SW	0.1
TEKNOLOGY PARTNERS INC	NW	0.1
AUGUSTINE ROOFING LLC	NE	0.2
DUMANIS SUPPORT SVC	NW	0.2
MESA LUNA RESTAURANT & BAKERY	SW	0.2
ATM	SW	0.2

Closest 50 locations   Page 1 of 8

Page 1 of 2

THE *Episcopal* CHURCH

St. Matthews Church (Sterling, VA) :
2260-0159
15 Minute Drive Time

EDUCATION

No High School Diploma	7%
High School Graduate (Including GED)	13%
Some College (Including Assoc Deg)	18%
Bachelor's Grad/Prof Degree	62%

LANGUAGE SPOKEN

English Only	58%
Spanish	15%
Indo-European	10%
Asian-Pacific Island	9%
Other Language	3%
Spanish & English Not Well	3%
Asian, Pacific Isl & English Not Well	1%
Indo-European & English Not Well	1%
Other Language & English Not Well	0%

(axis: 0, 40,000, 80,000, 120,000, 160,000)

MARITAL STATUS

Never Married	31%
Married	57%
Widowed	3%
Divorced	8%

(axis: 0%, 20%, 40%, 60%)

HAS A WORKING CELLPHONE

98%

ESRI TAPESTRY SEGMENTS

Tapestry Segments

2D Enterprising Professionals
35,617 households
35.0% of households

1C Boomburbs
13,184 households
13.0% of households

1B Professional Pride
11,550 households
11.4% of households

The lifestyle labels provided in the box above are proprietary labels created by Esri. The Episcopal Church recognizes that these may not be labels that would be endorsed by members of those groups. The information is included here because it provides valuable data on demographics. Its inclusion does not constitute endorsement of any of the labels.

LEARN More

If you would like access to more data, analytics, and demographic reporting, Datastory has established a discounted rate for the Episcopal Church.

Visit **https://www.datastoryconsulting.com/mapdash-faith** for more info.

If the average income in the neighborhood of this parish is $136,000, the average pledge is just shy of 4 percent of the average household income in that area. How does this compare with the national average? The Episcopal Church's data says that the average pledge in the Diocese of Virginia in 2018 was $3,200, so St. Matthew's should be pleased because they exceed the diocesan average in terms of dollars, although they've got a ways to go to meet the biblical standard of tithing. If the median household income in the state was $68,766, that average pledge of $3,200 represents 3.2 percent. This parish's average percentage is higher too. St. Matthew's seems to be doing good solid work inviting its members to support their ministry within and outside their walls. Not a tithe, but better than most. There's still work to be done to increase giving. But given that the average age at this parish is young, we shouldn't be surprised by that—it's usually the norm that younger families pledge a lower percentage than older givers. You could also do an average pledge calculation for a five-year spread and see if the average has tracked with the economy or has increased or decreased.

Last but not least, you can always go to your county website for demographic and income data (usually based upon US Census data). You might want to look at the demographics or you might want to look at data on rental housing in the community, which can be a fertile source of new parishioners.

Another set of data points for consideration has to do with endowments as a source of funding for operations or for capital projects. If a parish has a significant percentage of its operating budget supported by income from endowments rather than by pledge and loose-plate donations, it's not the healthiest of situations. This can happen for all sorts of reasons. Is this a church in a rural community with no economic growth, and the parishioners are "lifers" who are, one by one, departing for the Heavenly Banquet with no new parishioners to replace them? Or is this a place where parishioners' giving has not increased over time because there was always a sense that the endowments would keep the lights on and the priest paid? Is there a large building with high maintenance costs but used only four hours a week, and endowment income must pay for it? This information is important, and it may lead to some deep conversations about the sustainability of the parish, the way the community is the body of Christ and how money is a visible representation of that.

And the last set of numbers? It's "people" numbers, just as the number of parishioners on the rolls and the ASA are "people numbers." How many people have been baptized in the parish each year over the past several years? How many are children and how many are adults? How many have been confirmed or received? How many marriages? How many burials? How many people who are not members of the parish have been touched by your ministries? All of these numbers tell a story about parish life, evangelism, vitality, and opportunity.

So in St. Matthew's case, the ASA has been stable. The numbers of baptisms and confirmations have been stable following a period of higher growth in the early 2010s. Numbers of confirmands is much more variable, with some years in the double digits, some years less. What this may indicate is that there is a steady and solidly faithful push toward discipleship. There are no great big increases that might not be sustainable, but consistent work in the vineyards. If we were looking at a parish with steadily decreasing numbers, that might indicate a small community that is not growing, a sense of lack of welcome to newcomers, or some conflict in the parish that was blocking this element of growth. Or it might simply indicate a fallow period in the church's life . . . but it would be useful to try and figure out what is happening, because this will have an impact on the qualities you are looking for in your next priest.

Again: numbers are simply a snapshot in time that gives you the starting point for asking more questions about who you are as a parish. They are not intended to judge. They are simply intended to open the conversation about where you are, so you can consider where God wants you to be, and how you might get there. All of this information helps to shape the picture you present of your parish to potential candidates, and it is infinitely better to be clear and honest about your parish than to try and "fudge" things. In a survey of recently called clergy, the thing that was one of the most cited as a source of frustration was that they were not given a clear picture of the state of the parish's financial condition. Those numbers, and the other numbers described above, will help you be honest so that you can find a priest with the right gifts and graces to help your parish.

Question Three: "Who Are We Now, the (Beloved) Community?"

Parishes do not exist in a vacuum. They are situated in a community, a city, a town, a neighborhood, a county.

The question we're exploring now is whether the parish is in the community or of the community? What do we know about the community? How do we relate to the community?

Mapping the Parish

The starting point is a simple one: where do the parishioners live? It's a fascinating exercise to take a paper map and put pushpins where each parishioner lives, or do the virtual version of the same exercise with a tool like Google Maps, to see if parishioners live in the community or drive in from far away. Oftentimes, in older parishes, the tie to the church is familial rather than geographic—someone's grandparents attended this parish, and the children and grandchildren were baptized and married there, so they now attend, even though they no longer live in the neighborhood. In the Episcopal Church, the original model of attending a parish was based on your geography: if you lived in x area, you went to x parish. This was modeled after the Church of England structure: a parish was a territorial unit. Although a church would be within that territory (occasionally, more than one church), the parish was a place with defined boundaries.

That is no longer the case. Now, parishioners may drive past one or more Episcopal churches to get to "their" church. Their reasons for attending a particular church may be familial, a preference as to liturgical style, a place where friends attend, or a desire for a smaller family-style church rather than a large one, or vice versa. No one is required to attend the parish that is geographically close to their home.

So parishioners may come a distance to attend at a particular parish. The pushpins on the map may be spread over a twenty-mile radius, with most of them further out and only a few near the parish. The challenge, if a parish is largely made up of people who do not live in the parish community, is to live as part of that community because the parish is geographically located there.

Think, for example, of a parish in a neighborhood that is now economically blighted, or where the local folks are recent immigrants. There might be a significant socioeconomic difference between the parishioners and the locals. There might even be some fear. What about a large "downtown" church which is now surrounded by office buildings? There is no noncommercial or residential neighborhood there anymore. So *what* and *who* is the community and how does the parish interact with that community?

Windshield Survey

So how do we get a clearer picture of the community and how we interact with it? One method is a "windshield survey."

It can be as simple as driving around and taking note of what you see in the community. What is the housing like? Lots of private homes? Mostly older or historic homes? Any new construction? What does this tell you about the community? How might someone find resources in the community, like a doctor, an AA meeting, the drugstore? Are they visible or not? Are there resources in the neighborhood like restaurants, markets, libraries, medical facilities? Whom do you see on the streets? People who look like the parishioners in your pews, or people who do not? If so, in what way do they differ? Are there empty commercial spaces or abandoned properties, usually markers of economic stresses in the area? Does everyone shop in town or drive out to the Walmart on the edge of town? Do you recognize the names of the businesses because they are local longtime stalwarts, or because they're a branch of a national chain? Are there any local businesses? What schools do you see and what do they say about how the community cares for children? A cluster of old, poorly kept churches around a town square, with nothing but the name of the pastor and the worship schedule, may say that religious life is not very vibrant in the community. Look around the side of one of the buildings, however, and see a sign that says "Food Pantry open every Wednesday." At another church you see a Boy Scout troop trailer. And at yet a third, a sign advertising a Spanish language service at 1 p.m. each Sunday. Now the religious presence in the community looks a bit brighter, even if the buildings themselves are not. Perhaps this is a poorer community or an aging one, but there is mission going on here. See how your parish fits into your community, or if it does not, where the disconnect might be.

Mystery Worshipper

Now for something completely different: take a closer look at your own parish, but as a stranger. This requires some imagination, but you'll have some prompting questions that will assist you.

Imagine you are attending your parish for the first time. Let's say you did a website search for an Episcopal parish near your home and you decided to give it a try. We'll assume for the sake of this exercise that you were able to find the information you needed to get you to church at the right address and the right time (you may be surprised to realize that this isn't the case: more on your website later).

You drive up to the church. What do you see? Is it well-kept? Is the grass a foot high, and not because you're doing prairie reclamation? Do you see signs directing you to the parking area, and to the entrance to the church? Particularly in campuses with multiple buildings or entrances, it can be disconcerting if you cannot find the way in.

Once you find your way in, is there someone to direct you to the sanctuary? Are they friendly and helpful? Can you find a seat, or are folks carefully guarding their turf? Are there copies of the prayer book and hymnals in hand, or are there orders of service that contain the whole service?

Once you sit down, how full is the building? Did anyone welcome you personally? Is your pew comfortable? How would you describe the preservice atmosphere? What books does the congregation use during the service? What musical instruments are played? Did anything distract you?

Is the worship formal or relaxed? How would you describe it? High church/broad church/low church? Lots of music/little music/professional musicians did it all/congregation was encouraged to sing? Did you find the sermon satisfying? Which part of the service seemed most spiritually moving? And which part seemed least spiritually edifying?

How were strangers invited to coffee hour? How would you describe the after-service coffee?

If you were a stranger, how would you feel about making this church your regular place of worship, on a scale from 1 to 10 where 10 = ecstatic, 0 = no, thanks?

Anything you never noticed before at the church that makes you want to share it with the parish leadership?[8]

Why are we recommending this exercise? First of all, it helps identify your parish's strengths in welcoming the stranger, and this is useful information for the leadership. Second, it flags the less-than-perfect things that might be easy to fix (signage, for example). Third, it names "growing edges" that might require some particular skills of your next priest.

Communications

This encompasses the many ways your parish might be known in the community, in the diocese, in the world. It includes your internal communications (newsletters, e-mail blasts, and such) and your website, as well as your social media presence (Facebook, Twitter, Instagram, YouTube, for example).

Is your parish known through publicity around special events, like parish-wide yard sales, selling pumpkins, hosting farm tours? Are you known through publicity about services you offer the larger community, like ESL classes, Scout troops, a free clinic?

Links to news articles about your parish on your webpage are great ways of being present in your community.

Your diocesan transition ministry officer or your diocesan communications professionals might have suggestions and offer resources regarding your communications presence.

If your website is tired and is still listing Holy Week services on the home page when it's almost Pentecost, or if you have no website at all, an awareness of the workings of social media may be a particular gift you might look for in your next priest. It is a tool for evangelism for your parish.

The Work of Our Hands and Hearts

Most parishes have a number of programs, and people who support those programs. The altar guild, the music team, the acolyte leader, and the

---

8. This is a modified version of the "Mystery Worshipper" questionnaire on the "Ship of Fools" website. *https://shipoffools.com/mystery-worshipper/*. Although the reports on the website are often quite clever and funny—and sometimes downright depressing—the questions are quite revealing.

worship coordinator might all work with the priest to make sure worship is conducted well each Sunday, or the priest and the organist might do it all. There might be a superintendent of the Sunday school, and a team of volunteer teachers, or perhaps just one or two people lead Sunday school. Perhaps there are a few folks who tend to the buildings and grounds, either through a formal committee structure or through periodic parish workdays. Your task here is to list the various ministries present in your parish. It is also helpful to mention whether they are very active ministries, ones that are no longer very active, or ones that are simply a fond memory. You might also classify them as ones that are designed to serve those who are already members, and those that invite others into the knowledge and love of Christ and/or are a service to the larger community.

Asset Mapping

What are the gifts that are present in your parish? Do you have a great Sunday school program that runs well because of the dedicated and gifted volunteers? Do you have beautiful fellowship activities? Is yours a parish that has a wonderful music program because of its proximity to a nearby conservatory? Are you the place that helps people heal from a prior hurtful experience in a church?

One of the things you want to do as you prepare your profile or portfolio is to know your parish's gifts and graces, and an effective way to do that is to map your assets. You can explore this practice by putting your parish's assets on the church's Asset Map,[9] because you want to build upon and augment the assets you already have in your discernment of your next priest. An example: if you are a parish that has grown quickly and you have great energy, but your organizational structure doesn't reflect your needs, you might be seeking someone with gifts as an administrator. If you are a healthy parish full of retirees who now have the time to "go deep" in your spiritual reflection, you might want someone who has gifts in that area. If you are a small church in an area which will most likely see no growth, the gift that might be most helpful from your next priest is to thoughtfully and pastorally guide the parish in what the future might and might not look like.

---

9. *https://www.episcopalassetmap.org/.*

The purpose of this kind of information gathering is to know who your parish is, in itself and in its community, warts, beauty marks, and all. To know whom you might call, you need first to know who you are. Knowing your parish identity will help you ascertain, at least in part, where you might be going in the future, and that will help you see which candidate's gifts match the needs of the parish in the years to come. It also lays the groundwork for the strategic planning that every parish should do; it is time well-spent.

Mind the Gap: Bridging Information-Gathering between "Who Are We Now" and "Who Is God Calling Us to Be Next?"

Two powerful tools that are available to use to determine a great deal of information about the second and third questions of self-study are surveys and focus groups.

Surveys are a time-honored way of gathering data. You can ask demographic information, when folks joined the parish, what keeps them as members, what they like, what they don't like, what's important in their next priest, what their hopes and aspirations are for the parish—just about anything.

However, it is important to realize that while surveys can get lots of information, the longer the survey, the fewer people who will complete it. Focus your questions in ways that get you the information you most need. For example, imagine your parish is composed of faithful older parishioners who have been there for a long time and a group of newer young families. Are their desires and needs the same? Possibly not. Thus, you might want to be able to identify whether older parishioners respond differently than younger ones in terms of what is most important. You will need to identify the age bracket of the people who respond.

If in your research about how the parish sits in its community, you've determined that the community has changed around you and the parish is largely made up of people who drive in to church from a distance, you might want to ask questions that get people thinking about how the parish engages, serves, and invites the community.

If things haven't been going so well in the parish lately (conflict, declining membership or giving, nothing new or exciting going on), you might want to ask questions that invite people to dream about the future.

Make your questions clear, and if you're offering multiple options for answers, make them equally clear, unbiased, and understandable.

Consider how you will distribute the survey and receive it. Many parishes now put up their surveys in digital form on Google Docs or Survey Monkey. These are remarkably useful tools, offering you the ability to cross-tabulate results (how many newer parishioners came because of our website?) and giving quick reports of results. However, some less technologically savvy parishioners may need to have the survey in paper form, which will require adding that data by hand to the digital results.

One parish recently experimented with a series of mini-surveys—no more than ten questions per survey, each on a topic or ministry area, once a month for six months. They got very high participation given the brevity of the surveys, although they were not able to cross-tabulate based upon demographic data since they only asked for demographics on the first survey. Theirs was a relatively small congregation of mostly retirees—a homogeneous group—so demographics did not appear to be something important for them to track.

In the appendices, you will find several sample surveys. Don't simply duplicate one of these: ask yourself what questions do you need answers to, and which questions will get you that data.

Confidentiality is also very important. You want people to respond frankly. If you are doing an electronic survey, reassure members that no personal data will be associated with their responses and that you have no way of knowing who wrote what. Similarly, if you use paper surveys, do not ask participants to identify themselves. If there is a place to collect paper surveys, make sure it is a closed box that curious eyes cannot peek into. People need to feel trust to be fully honest in their responses. Make sure they can see and hear that confidentiality is a high priority for the group.

Some discernment committees offer the option for respondents to self-identify if they want to have a further (verbal) conversation with a member of the committee. If you offer that option, prepare to have those interviews relatively quickly after the survey is completed.

Do prepare the parish for the survey by introducing it in announcements, in newsletters and bulletins, and by making the rollout of the survey an event. Give a date for completion. Offer help if someone has limitations such as visual impairment that would make it difficult for them to participate. Make sure that members of the discernment committee are able to answer any questions parishioners might have. Celebrate if you have a high level of participation!

Once you have gathered your data, it is a good thing to share the results first with the vestry and then with the congregation at large. Some discernment committees simply summarize the results and others will do a full roll-up of the survey results, question by question (there is an example of one of these following the sample surveys). One parish even included the full details of their survey results as part of their description of the parish on their website. This shows remarkable transparency; it will be up to the discernment committee and the vestry to determine how your data is shared. Samples of surveys some parishes have devised in the past, as well as a sample survey roll-up, may be found in Appendix A.

Focus groups, or small group listening sessions, are another effective way of gathering information about the parish and its hopes, fears, and aspirations. The methodology is simple: gather small groups of people (not more than nine per group) and guide a conversation using a series of prompting questions. Someone will need to serve as a facilitator or convener, and another person will need to serve as a scribe to write down key words, themes, and ideas. As with all gatherings related to this process, prayer is the best way to begin, to remind all the participants that they are cocreating with God in this work. If your discernment committee has devised a prayer for the parish in this time of transition, share it, as well as the Lord's Prayer. Then, start with the questions. If yours is a large parish and members of the focus group don't know each other, it is helpful to ask initial questions such as "how long have you been a member?" or "what sort of activities do you participate in at church?" Then you might enter into questions that invite some thought. They should be open-ended, not yes-or-no, inviting the conversation to go where it will. The beauty of focus groups is that they have a life of their own. If the conversation takes a turn in a new direction, take it as the work of the Holy Spirit and let it meander a bit before bringing participants back to the question at hand. The scribe will be listening for and writing down words that continue to be repeated (it may be as obvious as "pastoral care" or "administrative" or "our kids" or as subtle as "kind" or "angry"—no word or theme is good or bad in and of itself, but may lead to further exploration of what the word means). The facilitator will know if the thread of conversation about a particular question is winding down, and may invite any final comments before moving on to the next question. Limit questions to a few, three or four at most. If people feel pressure to complete answering many questions, they will not delve as deeply into the sense and possibility inherent in each question.

Some sample questions:

"What makes our parish different from the others in this community?"

"If this parish shut its doors, what would be lost in this community?" (The negative version of the first question, it sometimes gets a stronger response.)

"How do we serve God here?"

"Are there things we should be doing to serve God that we haven't figured out yet?"

"What do we think this parish might look like five or ten years from now?"

"What do we think God has in mind for this place and for us in the years to come?"

"What sorts of gifts might we want in our next priest?" (This requires some delicacy to turn people away from their picture of the externals— young, attractive, married, kids—to their sense of their spiritual gifts— patient, clear, caring, teaching, connected to God.)

This is by no means a comprehensive list of the questions you might include in a focus group discussion, but it is a starting point.

If the focus groups have met as part of a larger parish gathering, do not have the groups report out in the "committee of the whole." Instead, gather what the scribes for each focus group have written. Look for common themes. You want to see the shared experiences, hopes, and fears of the group. This data will not only give you a clear picture of the parish as it is today, but will give you a sense of where the Spirit may be leading the parish next, as well as the gifts your next priest will need to help the parish get there. A more detailed set of guidelines for the conduct of focus groups can be found in Appendix B.

Appreciative Inquiry Congregational Meeting is a remarkably efficient way to do this sort of work in very small congregations. The process is based on the notion that it is easiest for us to talk about our parish when we start with what we most love/appreciate about it. This process identifies themes around the parish's hopes and aspirations as a place where God's work is done that can effectively guide answering the questions that will be in the community ministry portfolio. A sample format for a congregational meeting in this style can be found in Appendix C.

Preparing the Community Ministry Portfolio

You have gathered all the data. You've discussed what gifts might be the primary ones you will seek in your next priest. It's time to bring that information together in the primary tool to share this opportunity with potential candidates: the community ministry portfolio. This document will reside in the database of the Office of Transition Ministry for the Episcopal Church. Priests who are seeking new calls use this as a resource to identify parishes in search. There will be other ways you will promote your search, but all rely on this database.

This document contains some "nuts and bolts" information relating to the parish. Much of that data can be made available to you by the vestry. It offers the chance to showcase the parish's web and social media presence. It gives key contact information. But the most interesting part of the CMP is a series of narrative questions.

These questions are designed to tease out how you operate as a church community. Some are fairly straightforward: a question about liturgical practices gives you the chance to say "we are deeply committed to the Anglo-Catholic tradition of formal worship with chanting and incense" or "so many of us come from other traditions that our common ground is the beautiful hymns that are in *Lift Every Voice and Sing*," or "We do Rite I without music at 8 a.m., then a family-friendly and noisy service at 9:45 with everything from bluegrass to Taizé, then a more formal Rite II service at 11:30 with organ and full choir, mostly singing from the Anglican tradition and *Hymnal 1982*." Other questions will get you thinking: "How are you preparing for the church of the future?" Some questions might make you a little nervous: "What is your experience of conflict?" Answer these questions from your hearts and tell the truth. Each congregation is a tapestry with bright and shining colors and dark and shadowy ones. Only telling about the happy times means you don't get to tell about those moments when the parish struggled and found the strength through God's grace to be resilient and creative. If you say that your church has had no experience of conflict, candidates will wonder what you're hiding, because every church has conflict. It's part of our nature as human beings and it's part of any institution that there will be disagreements and different approaches. Just as change is inevitable, reaction to change is also inevitable, so tell your story.

Occasionally, committees or vestries will be afraid of airing past struggles, thinking it will "scare off" candidates. If a candidate is scared off by the truth of your story, they are not the right candidate. Most priests know the complexity of the human condition and how it plays out in parish life. This is borne out in doctoral research with priests in the Diocese of Virginia relating to the transition process. Most identified some issue that the committee or the vestry did not share with them prior to their acceptance of the call. When asked if they would have taken the call had they known about the issue, every one of them said, "I still would have taken that call, but I would have begun my work in the parish differently." Let candidates know the fullness of who you are, your hopes and dreams and your worries, so that your mutual discernment will be grounded in truth and love.

Some practical aspects of responses to these questions: the text block for each of the answers to the narrative questions is strictly limited to 1,200 characters, including spaces and punctuation. There is no wiggle room. This may feel overly limiting, but look at these brief answers as an invitation to a conversation, not a telling of the whole story. One of the questions invites naming no more than four qualities you seek in your next priest. There is only space for two or three words for each quality, so prioritize what is most important and share it briefly.

There is a blessing in disguise in this series of questions. Priests fill out a database form that has questions that will parallel your CMP. Your committee can see how they respond and this will provide clues to how the priest thinks and how it might align with your parish. If a priest is deeply committed to social justice ministry and that features prominently in their answers to questions, and you are seeking a priest with a heart for pastoral care in your aging congregation, it invites priests to consider "would I be happy here?" If that priest applies, you are able to ask the question "how does your obvious passion for social justice ministry align with our desire to call a priest who will walk with us as pastor as we age?" A priest whose liturgical bent is Anglo-Catholic might not be happy in a parish that is more low church in its liturgical expression, or one where people claim that incense gives them migraines.

In Appendix D, committees will find a document providing an overview of the community ministry portfolio and how to fill it out. There is also a document that explains the details of clergy compensation, which differs in key ways from secular compensation.

It's Done!

Once you have completed a draft, you will want vestry approval before your community ministry portfolio is posted on the database. In many dioceses, this draft is reviewed by the transition ministry officer to catch any idiomatic language that might have a particular meaning to priests that might be used in a different way by a lay writer. It's also an opportunity for the transition ministry officer to say, "You might want to approach this a little differently." Generally, the TMO can imagine how what you've written will land on the ears of candidates, and while we always want the CMP to be written in the voice of YOUR parish, we also can head off any misunderstandings with a few gentle edits.

If your vestry becomes concerned with truth-telling in the CMP— "You're airing our dirty laundry!"—tell them about the power of sharing the whole tapestry of your story, the stories of resilience and growth in the midst of challenge as well as the glory days, so that your next priest will not be surprised once they begin.

Promoting Your Position

Filling out the community ministry portfolio is the first step in letting the world know you are interested in applicants. Priests who are considering a new call will regularly check the national database to see which parishes are currently receiving names of applicants. Most dioceses post openings in their diocese on their website. Some regional groups of transition ministry officers meet periodically to share opportunities, since we are often aware of priests who are seeking a new call for whom there is no right call in our own diocese. Priests are ordained for the whole church, not just one's original diocese, so to the extent a priest is free to seek a call outside a diocese's boundaries (and bishops will generally support a priest's desire to take a call outside of the diocese), sharing calls and names of priests is a normal thing. Most transition ministry officers will send an e-mail to the listserv of TMOs, promoting the position. In recent years, many positions have been advertised on the Episcopal News Service digital job board. Frequently, though, the way that candidates find out about positions is through their friends and colleagues in ministry. The network of Episcopal clergy is remarkably tight-knit, and if there is a position in my diocese that I know my friend who serves in Spokane would be interested in, I let her know. This is common practice throughout the church.

You may discover that parishioners know of potential candidates. This will be dealt with in more depth in the next section, but it is cleaner and easier if you are not the "headhunter," but tell that parishioner who collars you on Sunday to tell you about their sister's cousin's priest in Ashtabula this: "That's wonderful! Please do let the priest know our parish is in search. You can invite the priest to check out the CMP and see if the Holy Spirit is nudging them toward discerning with us." Then if the priest discerns no sense of call, it is the priest's decision and not a failing of the committee that this is not the next priest.

On to the next phase of the process!

VIII

―――――◆―――――

FOR THE VESTRY:
PHASE TWO

At this point, the discernment committee will have completed the work of self-study. They will have developed your parish's community ministry portfolio, which you will review. Remember that you have delegated the responsibility for this work to the discernment committee, so your review should be for accuracy of data rather than for editing for content. You may be surprised by what your parishioners have told the committee: prior to their work, there may not have been an opportunity to have conversations about the parish's hopes and dreams. We urge you to avoid the temptation to say, "Well, that's not what this parish is about! You've got it wrong." It may simply be that your parish has a wider range of opinions, hopes, dreams, and challenges than you were aware of, and it's a gift when people feel safe enough to share that information. God is always doing a new thing, and this is when it's particularly important to hear about that through the voices of your parishioners and your discernment committee.

Pay particular attention to the gifts and graces and skills that your committee has said are the highest priorities for candidates. Remember that all priests have at least a baseline competency in all the work that priests are called to do. Priests also have some strengths and some areas which are not quite as strong. That is why your discernment committee will look for particular strengths to respond to the parish's needs at this time. It is fair game to ask them why they've named these gifts as the priorities. It is not fair game to try to change those priorities to respond to your personal needs or opinions rather than those of the parish. You're seeking God's will for the *parish*, after all!

Once the community ministry portfolio is approved by the vestry, your transition minister will publish it on the database (*www.otmportfolio.org*). That database is only accessible by priests. Notice that you are receiving names will also be published on your diocese's website. In most dioceses, the transition ministry officer will send an e-mail to the nationwide network of diocesan transition ministers, who will share it with priests seeking new calls in their dioceses. It may also be posted on the digital job board of the Episcopal News Service (*https://www.episcopalnewsservice.org/jobs/*). Regional gatherings of transition professionals are also times when your parish's need for a new priest will be shared. Depending on the level of experience you seek from your next ordained leader, you might also contact Episcopal seminaries.

How long will your discernment committee receive names? The norm is four to six weeks. If that stage of your process bridges Holy Week or Christmas, the "receiving names" period should be extended for a couple weeks more, since priests are very busy at that time of the year and may not have time to focus on new possibilities. If by some chance the discernment committee feels they do not have a robust enough pool of candidates, the time period of receiving names may be extended very easily.

This leads to the subject of numbers of applicants. As has been written elsewhere in this book, parishes do not get the large number of applicants that they used to. This is a nationwide phenomenon. There is good news in this, though: those who do apply have a clearer picture of what your parish seeks (those gifts/graces/skills) so the quality of the candidate pool in response to those needs will be higher. Some parishes may have received five applications, some may have received ten. No recent openings have yielded more than thirty applications, and that's fine.

This is also the time when "the cone of silence" descends. Your discernment committee will be receiving applications, but they cannot tell you anything about those applications. Nothing about numbers, nothing about demographics, nothing about geographic distribution. Nothing.

Part of your responsibility during this period is to protect your discernment committee from inappropriate inquiries regarding candidates. Well-meaning but anxious parishioners might approach the committee—make sure you say that the best thing that parishioners can do to support the search is to keep praying. As was mentioned before, if a parishioner suggests a potential candidate, encourage them to contact the candidate and tell them to check out your parish's website and community ministry portfolio on the OTM database and see if they feel called to apply.

The committee will not only be interviewing candidates either via videoconferencing or in person, they will also be traveling (two or three committee members on such a trip) to see finalists in their current ministry setting. You will have already budgeted funds to cover this cost. They may bring finalists to your locale so that the whole committee can interview them in person. Remember, though, that you will not meet them at this time. Only when they have decided on the priest they will be recommending and after all the final steps of due diligence have been completed will you be given their name. At that point, you will be briefed by the committee about the candidate and you will enter the final phase of the process.

Remember that your ability to lead with prayerful calm will influence the whole parish's ability to trust in the process and those who are doing the work. God's time is not our time, and the candidate will come. Trust and pray, and then pray some more. All shall be well!

IX

FOR THE DISCERNMENT COMMITTEE: PHASE TWO AND FINAL STEPS

Your community ministry portfolio has been published, and you are now starting to receive names. What happens now?

Confidentiality

First, you have now entered into work where confidentiality is paramount. You cannot share information about candidates, not even the number of applicants or where they come from, with *anyone*, including the vestry. You are holding priests' careers in your hands. Do not tell anyone anything.

Discerning Gifts

Second, this work of evaluating and discerning which candidates align with the parish's needs is holy ground. It is to be done prayerfully, with an eye to the gifts you articulated as those the parish needs rather than things like physical attractiveness, gender, marital status, or any other external variables. Remember God's warning to Samuel as he sought the next king of Israel: "Do not look on his appearance or on the height of his stature, because I have rejected him; for the Lord does not see as mortals see; they look on the outward appearance, but the Lord looks on the heart" (1 Sam. 16:7).

Hold Your Opinions Lightly

Remember, too, that although you may have a particular preference for a particular reason, you are not looking for *your* priest, you are seeking the *parish's* priest.

The Spiritual Nature of the Work You Do

Remember the Golden Rule

You touch the hopes, dreams, and ministry of each member of the clergy with whom you are in conversation, whether or not they get an interview. How you treat them, their family, and work situations provides an opportunity to love your neighbor as you love yourself.

Take Time for Prayer

Prayer guides us throughout this process, but it needs to be central to your vetting process. It's good to halt conversation and ask that the discernment committee takes time to pray. It's all right to say that you all need more time in prayer together or separately before you make your next decision. Begin each meeting with a Bible study or read a reflection, if you're not doing so already.

Some Passages for Reflection
- Sharing leadership (Num. 11:16–17, 24–25a),
- Discernment and the variety of gifts (Rom. 12:1–18),
- Sources of recommendation and qualification (2 Cor. 3:1–9),
- Jesus's prayer for the church (John 17:15–21),
- God's call to holiness (1 Pet. 1:13–21).

Prayer for Guidance

O God, by whom the meek are guided in judgment, and light rises up in darkness for the godly: Grant us, in all our doubts and uncertainties, the grace to ask what you would have us to do, that the Spirit of wisdom may save us from all false choices, and that in your light we may see light, and in your straight path we may not stumble; through Jesus Christ our Lord. *Amen.* (BCP, 832)

Receiving Names

You will receive applications from candidates. These applications should include a cover letter, their OTM (Office of Transition Ministry, the church's database) portfolio, and a resume. Send them an e-mail to say that you've received their application and will be in touch as you consider the applications.

There is usually an initial screening of candidates, particularly if they come from outside your diocese, by your transition ministry officer, although a few diocesan TMOs do this later in the process. The chair of the committee should send an e-mail to your TMO to do an initial reference check on each candidate. If the candidate comes from within your diocese, your TMO will already know the priest well and can give you initial impressions of strengths and growing edges. If the candidate comes from outside your diocese, the TMO will contact their counterpart in that diocese. The concerns at this point are issues that might disqualify a candidate for consideration—"baggage," if you will—that would mean that they would not be suitable. Sometimes those issues might relate to medical, emotional, or behavioral struggles. Sometimes there might be a question as to whether or not the priest is the right fit. For example, a priest with a management style that is highly controlling might not suit a parish that prefers a very collaborative style. A priest who has acted in ways that led to conflict in their last call is a concern. Some of these matters are immediately disqualifying, some are not. The diocesan transition ministry officer will share as much as possible, but occasionally may simply say "please take Candidate X off your list" because they are limited in what they are allowed to say about the issues at play. This is not done casually, or because of personal preference but because there is history that leads to the conclusion that the priest would bring unhealthy behaviors to the parish and the diocese.

Don't Worry about the Number of Applicants

In 2015, one of our diocese's largest churches—with about 500 people on a Sunday and a million dollar plus budget—received fewer than thirty applicants for their open position. Twenty years ago, the same church likely would have received 150 applicants. The trend across the church, in every region and diocese, is that fewer people are applying for open positions. There are a few reasons why this is likely happening. One is that two-income families are the norm now, and the spouses of clergy typically make more money than the priest, so it makes less financial sense to move the family for the priest to take a new job.

This can worry some committees, but there's little to be done about it. The upside is that the committee spends less time wading through unqualified candidates, and candidates are more likely to feel an authentic sense of call to serve the church. Your transition ministry officer can let you know if the number of applicants tracks with the average for a church of your size and compensation level.

Initial Winnowing

You will then start to review the applications as a committee, seeing how they align with the committee's priorities in terms of gifts/skills/attributes. Note, though, that gifts sometimes come in packages that do not fit what you imagine the package should look like—age, gender, marital status, ethnicity, for example—but do recall that it is the gifts you should care about. The package that those gifts are wrapped in is not important.

Through much discernment, prayer, and work, you have uncovered the church's priorities and articulated them in your community ministry portfolio. It's important that your priorities remain your guiding light (for example, a priest might be charming, but is she pastoral? He may be warm and friendly, but can he manage a church of your size?).

At this stage, you should also ignore any information that they give vis-à-vis their desired compensation. Since compensation is so dependent on cost of living in any locale, it can be a distraction. Assume, at this stage, that the priest would not have applied if they did not consider what you say is the compensation available for your position to be within their range of reasonability.

Consider the Candidates in Three Categories

- Aligns perfectly with what we said we were looking for.
- Mostly aligns with what we said we were looking for.
- Does not align at all with what we said we were looking for.

Send a note to those who are in the last category, thanking them for applying but saying in a kind way that the parish is looking for someone with different gifts than those they offer. It is no kindness to keep a priest hanging on indefinitely if there is no chance you will ever call them.

First Stage Interviewing

Before You Schedule

You know you will want to do an initial interview with those in the "aligns perfectly" category. Once you have heard from your transition ministry officer whether or not you can proceed with each of those candidates based on the initial reference check, you can schedule interviews—a reference is usually available within forty-eight hours, depending on the response time from out-of-diocese counterparts.

Videoconferencing First

Usually, unless the candidates are local, first interviews are done using Skype, GoToMeeting, or Zoom. Whether you interview in person or using a videoconferencing tool like those mentioned above, your interview protocol should be the consistent with each candidate. You want to do an "apples to apples" comparison between the candidates.

Come up with a few questions that probe how the candidate lives into the gifts that you've said you want. For example, if you say you want a priest who can improve the culture of stewardship, encouraging joyful and generous giving, you might say, "Tell us about how you have encouraged giving in your current call. How would you help us see giving not as a painful obligation but as a way to increase our ability to do mission and ministry?"

It is usually impossible to cover more than three or four questions in that initial interview of an hour or so. Remember that the candidates, in filling out their OTM profiles, will have answered questions that parallel the ones you answered when you developed your community ministry portfolio, so you will already have many insights into how they think and how well that matches how you've described your parish.

You can certainly ask questions if there was something in their application that made you curious, or if their responses to one of your questions seemed unusual and you want clarification.

You're looking for real, lived experience. Occasionally nervous candidates might launch into their philosophy or theology of whatever you're asking. That's not helpful. For example, I might have a philosophy of Christian formation for children that says it must be experiential, joyful, and flexible, but I might not actually be able to choose, design, and implement such a program. Gently redirect candidates toward stories of their experience that demonstrate their competence or their learnings. Watch what they get excited about, what they think is most important, where they show joy in the work.

Leave some time for the candidate to ask you questions. This is mutual discernment, not a hiring process. It's more like finding a life partner than hiring a new VP of Sales, so both parties are seeking to learn more about each other.

Who Asks What

Some committees choose to assign different members to ask each question. It's a good idea to have someone take notes for future reference, when you start to consider which of the candidates you want to keep in consideration and which do not seem to fit the bill.

Discerning Next Steps

After you have completed this round of interviews, consider which ones should continue in discernment with you. Consider, too, if any of the candidates from the middle category (the "interesting possibility despite the fact that they don't check all the boxes" group) are feeling like ones whom you should also interview.

Once all the interviews in this round are done, it's time for prayer and discernment to figure out who advances to the next round.

Behavioral Interview Guide

Another way to frame the questions you will ask is called "behavioral interviewing." It is intended to draw out information about the candidate's competence or skill in a particular area. This approach is based on what is called the "STAR" method. The STAR method asks the candidate to discuss the specific situation, task, action, and result of the situation you are describing.

Situation: The candidate must describe a specific event or situation, not a generalized description of what has been done in the past. Ask for details. This situation does not necessarily have to be in the priest's present call, but should be relatable to parish ministry.

Task: What was it that the priest was trying to accomplish or complete? What portion was the direct work of the priest and what was directed by the priest for others to do?

Action: What did the priest do?

Result: What was the result? It is legitimate for the result to be negative, and it actually may reveal more about the priest's capacity to flex, to learn, to plan ahead for the next time than a purely positive story.

There are a variety of things you may want to know about, but your primary focus is always on the gifts or skills you have identified as the most important ones on your CMP. The recipe for the question has three parts:

1. Start the question with a positioning statement:
    a. In your work at . . .
    b. All of us have gone through times when things didn't go as planned . . .
    c. Now let's focus on . . .

2. Include an open-ended phrase that invites a story:

    a. Tell us about a time when . . .

    b. Give us an example of . . .

    c. Tell us about a recent . . .

    d. Describe a project that . . .

3. Close the loop on the event:

    a. What did you do?

    b. How did it turn out?

Evaluating Candidates' Answers

These may be some less-than-stellar answers you encounter:

Vague Statements

Q: "What actions have you taken to keep your preaching at its best?"

A: "They start to wiggle if I run longer than eleven minutes, so my primary job is to keep it short."

Q: "Tell us about a time when you felt overwhelmed in your ministry. What action did you take to get some relief? What difference has it made in your life, if any?"

A: "I never had that problem."

Opinions

Q: "Tell us about a recent staff meeting that you led in which personal agendas dominated. How did you intervene? How did it turn out?"

A: "I don't think there is a place for personal opinions at staff meetings. They are for one-on-one meetings."

Q: "What actions have you taken to make your church's vision or mission meaningful to members? What has worked and what has not?"

A: "It is so important that everyone understand the church's mission and live into it."

Theoretical or Future Tense Statements

Q: "Would you share with us an experience you had with a lay leader that was extremely difficult to handle. What was the situation, what did you do, and how did it turn out?"

A: "Once I got some heat from a vestry member about whether or not AA could use the parish hall. Next time I'll know how to handle it."

Q: "How has your personal theology shaped your professional and personal life?"

A: "I promised myself that I would read the Daily Office every day and I intend to do it."

If you get an incomplete or unsatisfying answer, it is fair to ask a follow-up question.

- Rather than talking to us about a philosophy of responding to the problem, what did you actually do?
- Walk us through the process step-by-step explaining what your role was.
- I understand what Mrs. Smith did. Help me understand what part you played.
- Interesting! Why did you . . .

Note that you will not be able to cover everything you wish you could cover, but trust your instincts. If something doesn't sound authentic or complete, your sense of the candidate may give you all the information you need. Know, too, that this isn't a "third degree." A candidate may be nervous or may not quite understand your question. Be gentle, but get the information you need!

Some Questions Clergy Might Ask You

1. How does this parish live the gospel?
2. Name three ways in which this parish encourages ministry.
3. How will this parish reveal love for my spouse and/or my family?
4. To what future is God calling this community?

5. How does this parish live out "the Apostles' teaching and fellowship, the breaking of bread and the prayers"?

6. What is of essential value to the life of this community? What would you never let go?

7. How does this community live its life of prayer?

8. What are the parish resources like, in people and in finance?

9. What issues exist for this congregation?

10. What do you believe calls me to possible ministry in this place?

11. Are there critical issues of historical importance for this place?

12. What do you most appreciate about one another?

13. What mission that you haven't yet explored exists for this congregation?

14. What kind of risks do people in this parish take for the sake of the gospel?

15. How do you communicate?

16. What's the "third rail"?

17. What would I have to do to get fired here?

Short-List Work

When you've narrowed your list down to two or three candidates, call your transition ministry officer to request background checks.

Depending on the practice in your diocese, it can take some time to get these checks completed. Coordinate with your transition ministry officer to determine when the TMO will expect that process to be completed.

Conduct Reference Checks

A candidate's OTM profile will always list their bishop and the transition ministry officer in their diocese. You won't call them, but you can go ahead and call anyone else they list on the OTM profile or resume as a reference.

If you get a lukewarm response from a reference, ask if he/she has contact information for someone else who might give you a picture of the candidate's work. The reference might just be having a bad day or they might be withholding part of the story.

You should also do a Google search; you might get a broader picture of the priest that way. If by any chance you find something disturbing, first verify that it is the same person. If it is indeed the same person, let your transition ministry officer know immediately.

"Pre-Flight Check"

You will send teams (two or three persons) of committee members to visit candidates in their current ministry location. Before committee members begin visiting candidates' parishes, touch base with your transition ministry officer to make sure the candidates have been vetted sufficiently to go ahead. You don't want to spend money traveling to see candidates who might have been disqualified.

On the Road: Visiting Candidates in Their Own Parish

Use this guide after the initial interviews and spending time as a committee in discernment and conversation following the interviews. It's not required, but the committee may feel it's necessary to do a second set of interviews before starting in on parish visits.

Two or Three Finalists

We recommend that your shortlist be two or three finalists. Any more can make parish visits take much longer; and faithful, in-depth discernment is more difficult with more candidates.

Update the Finalists

Let the finalists know they have proceeded to the next level of the discernment process. One committee sent out this e-mail:

> *Dear (name) The St. Swithen's Discernment Committee decided last night that we would like to send a couple of members of the committee to visit with you and hear you preach. We are looking at either Sunday June 1 or Sunday June 8. Would either or both of these dates work for you? I'd like to have a*

phone conversation with you about details, but first I wanted to let you know the decision of the committee and the possible dates for a visit so we can begin to get organized. We're excited that our discernment process is moving along!

God's blessings to you,
[Discernment Committee Chair]

Releasing Nonfinalists

If you haven't done so already, let the nonfinalists know that they're not the right fit. Depending on the amount of time and energy the priest has invested in the process so far, you will likely want to do them the courtesy of calling to give this news.

In the world of secular employment, employers typically won't give details as to why they went in a different direction due to fear of saying the wrong thing and opening themselves up to a lawsuit. However, we're not subject to the same restrictions of the business world: it's permissible to let priests know why you went in another direction, as long as you are kind. It will be helpful to them in their discernment.

Decide Whom You'll Send

We recommend sending no more than two or three people to see the candidate in action. It may be appropriate to send a fourth person if it's a large parish or the parish knows the candidate is in search. But, particularly if they are serving a small parish, it can be difficult to fly under the radar screen. If there are two of you, you can sit together. If there are three, do not sit together. If anyone asks you, you are simply passing through and wanted to go to an Episcopal church service that Sunday. It's important to do your best to not look like you're scouting out the priest.

Discernment committee members cannot bring family or friends with them to the service, whether or not they attend your church.

Lunch or Dinner

You may want to go out to dinner with the candidate the night before or to lunch afterwards. Have the candidate suggest a place where it's unlikely you all will run into parishioners. It's great to have a more casual time to get to know the candidate (and their spouse, if they are married).

Reporting Out

Make sure the "travel teams" from the committee can report coherently and clearly to the search committee as a whole. Since everyone won't be able to visit, it's important that the visitors be able to paint a good picture.

Visit Checklist

Have a list of things you're looking for that you can make notes about—afterwards, not at the church. Having a common list of things that all search committee visitors look for will help the discernment committee compare candidates.

Your Observations Should Cover:

Preaching

Did the sermon connect to the gospel and to your daily life? Did it seem relevant? Was it too heady or too folksy? What did you think of the delivery?

Remember that good preachers can adjust their delivery depending on the context.

Liturgical Style

What did you notice about how the priest does worship?

Was it reverent, joyful, or maybe a little stiff? Could you feel that these were more than just words for the priest?

But remember, not everything a priest does is necessarily their choice—it may be that way because of the parish's customs rather than because of personal preference.

For example, if you dislike when the candidate chanted part of the Eucharistic Prayer, that may not have been the priest's choice—it may have "always been that way" and the priest does it because it's meaningful to that parish.

Interaction with the Parish

Is she warm/welcoming or reserved? Do parishioners seek her out to share stories?

Is the candidate a "child magnet" with the kids of the parish running up to talk to her or get a hug?

If it is clearly a church that is dying, how does the candidate support them with love and dignity?

If there are quirky or difficult people, how does the priest interact with them?

How does the priest's story intertwine with the church's story?

Other

Have your list of priorities close at hand. Certain priorities like "congregational development" might not be observable on a Sunday, but, for example, if children's ministry is a priority, you will want to take note of how children are incorporated in the service, if there's a children's sermon, etc.

Take a Bulletin with You

You can learn a lot about a parish from its bulletin, and you can show it to the rest of the discernment committee if it has points of interest.

Make a List of Questions for the Priest

If you thought a liturgical practice was strange, or didn't understand a reference in their sermon, or thought the delivery was a little too lively or complacent for your church, it's all right to ask the priest about it. Your questions will be informative for you and the priest, and give you a sense of what is their personal style and what's an adaptation based on local custom.

Thank the Candidate

Express gratitude for their willingness to welcome the discernment committee members into their community after the visit, with a mention of when they might hear if they will be considered to go forward in the discernment.

You might say, "We've got one other person to visit next Sunday, then the committee will meet together the following week to discern which candidates we'd like to continue to discern with."

If the Candidate Isn't Serving a Parish

If a candidate isn't serving at a parish, see if they can line up a date to serve as a supply priest elsewhere. The priest should arrange this, not the committee. While it's not as ideal as seeing the candidate in their own ministry setting, it will still allow the committee to see the priest preach and function liturgically.

It's not always a red flag that someone doesn't have a job: They could be returning to ministry after spending time with their children, they could have just moved to the area because their spouse found a job, or they could have finished up a call that was for a specific amount of time.

For the Discernment Committee: Final Phase

When You've Found "The One"

1. **Call the finalist** and ask if they still want to be presented as the final candidate to the vestry.

2. **Call your transition ministry officer** to say which candidate is going to be presented. We will have already ordered the background check, by the way, but it will take a little while to process. Until you get the go-ahead from your transition ministry officer, you cannot share the name of the finalist with the vestry. The TMO will tell the bishop about your recommendation.

3. **Bishop-to-bishop call:** If the candidate is from out of your diocese, your bishop will call the candidate's bishop—it may feel pro forma, but bishops rightfully are sticklers about such things. The bishop may also call the candidate or meet in person with them to get a sense of the priest and to discuss priorities. Again, this is something that must be done before the candidate's name can be presented. Sometimes it takes a little time for the bishops to coordinate their schedules to have such a phone call. Be patient!

4. **Go-ahead from transition office:** Once that happens, and once the background check is done, the TMO will tell you that the committee can present the candidate to the vestry.

5. **Brief the vestry:** It is usually helpful for the committee to give the vestry a briefing book to prepare them to meet the candidate. This might include the process you used, the sorts of questions you asked, the sorts of answers given, observations of your visit, etc. What led you all to discern that this priest was indeed "the one"? That is what the vestry will most want to hear.

6. **Discharge:** Once you have presented her/him to the vestry, you may be discharged from your duties as the search committee.

7. **Vestry meeting:** The vestry will invite the candidate to come and meet with them. They will interview the candidate and will vote to affirm your recommendation (or not, but that's very rare) and they will be responsible for notifying the bishop (via your transition ministry officer) that they have voted to elect this person as your next rector, and they will negotiate the letter of agreement.

Please note: it is likely that the vestry is getting pretty anxious to meet the candidate by this point, and they may be pushing hard to get moving. Do not allow yourselves to let their impatience become your anxiety. You cannot present the candidate to the vestry until your transition ministry officer says the due diligence is completed.

X

For the Vestry: Final Steps

The discernment committee has discerned the candidate which they want to present to the vestry, the final steps are done (background check, bishop-to-bishop call, bishop-to-candidate call) and they are ready to present their recommended candidate to you. They *cannot* do this until your transition ministry officer tells them that the due diligence is completed and they are free to present the candidate to you.

1. We recommend that the discernment committee give the vestry a briefing book to prepare them to meet the candidate. This might include the processes the discernment committee used, the sorts of questions that were asked, the sorts of answers given, observations of their visit, etc. The discernment committee is asked to say what led them all to discern that this priest was indeed "the one." Once the discernment committee has presented the candidate, the vestry may discharge them from their duties.

2. The vestry will then reach out to the candidate to schedule a time when the candidate can come to meet with you for an interview. The purpose of this interview is to get to know the candidate (and spouse, if that is the priest's situation), to confirm that they do, indeed, bring the gifts that you have named in your community ministry portfolio as the priorities in the next chapter of the parish's story, and how you might define priorities in the work to come—in short, to get a sense of how you might work together.

3. After that, the vestry will vote whether or not to affirm the discernment committee's recommendation (it's quite rare for a vestry to decide against a candidate, by the way, but if the vestry feels the discernment committee has missed the mark, it's time to call the transition ministry officer and figure out what's happening).

4. If the vote is to affirm, you call the candidate and tell them you would like to call them as the next rector. They will say yes or no (sometimes they ask for a day or two of prayer before they say yes—don't be disturbed by this because it is not uncommon). Assuming they say yes, notify the bishop through your transition ministry officer and you begin your work of negotiating the letter of agreement.

5. PLEASE NOTE THAT YOU CANNOT ANNOUNCE THE CALL UNTIL THE LETTER OF AGREEMENT IS SIGNED BY ALL PARTIES, INCLUDING THE BISHOP, if that is the practice in your diocese.

6. Most dioceses have templates for letters of agreement. If you have questions about the "nuts and bolts" of this part of the work, please call your transition ministry officer for a review. Once the vestry and candidate have a mutually agreeable draft, send it to the transition ministry officer. They will review it one last time, and if it is as it should be, affirm that the senior warden and the priest may sign it. Send a scanned copy to your transition ministry officer and the TMO will have the bishop sign it, if that is your diocese's practice.

7. Timing of when the priest begins their new call is a point of negotiation. Although you are excited and anxious for this wonderful priest to begin with you, be reasonable. Two weeks is insufficient notice to a parish that is just learning their priest is leaving—it does not allow for the "good goodbye" discussed in the beginning of this book. A month at the very least, perhaps two, seems to work well in most cases.

8. Once the letter of agreement is signed by the bishop, an announcement of the call may be made. Please note that you should coordinate the announcement in your parish with the announcement the priest will be making in her/his own parish. It's not fun or fair for one parish to get

good news and the other one get an inadvertent surprise that will set them on their heels.

9. If, anywhere along the way on this stage of the journey, you have concerns or questions, please let the transition ministry officer know—it is their mission to help make this as smooth as possible.

One More Goodbye: To Your Interim Rector

Just as you had a "good goodbye" with your last rector, if you have had an interim, now is the time to plan a farewell to that faithful temporary shepherd. Much of the same principles apply, with certain key differences:

- On occasion, interims have had to do some hard work getting the parish prepared for the next priest. Not everyone may have been happy about the changes that were necessary. It is always helpful to name the areas that were painful but necessary steps. It is like the prep work we sometimes have to do before medical procedures—we want the best result possible, so we do the tough stuff so we are ready.
- The same rules apply vis-à-vis departing interims as apply to departing priests: no coming back for funerals, weddings, baptisms except under the most extraordinary circumstances, and only with the prior approval of the new rector.
- Any accrued and unused vacation time should be paid out promptly.
- A farewell with a thank-you party is a great idea.

Welcoming Your New Priest

Work Space

You may think that your new priest's office is just fine. After all, it looks just it did when the former occupant was there. But consider this: your last priest was six feet tall, rarely used the desktop computer, and only wanted a comfortable chair to sit in when a parishioner was meeting with him. Your new priest may have different needs, or time may have taken its toll. The room is still painted the same industrial green as it was when the last priest was called. There are brown spots on the acoustic tile where the bathroom above leaked.

Now is the time to prepare the work space where your new priest will do their desk work, meet with parishioners, and plan for the next meeting.

If there are things that need repair or replacement, like ceiling tiles or the blinds that are locked into a single height and cannot be adjusted, attend to that. Clean the carpet or repair the floor if necessary.

If there are bookshelves, make sure they are cleared. Sometimes these shelves become repositories for books that are no longer used or have no home. This is a good time to determine if there is a use for them or if they should go away. That space is where your priest will put their library, and it's an occupational hazard that we priests have a lot of books, and the office is the logical place to keep most of them. If the bookshelves need repair or repainting, attend to that.

Check with the priest if they have a preference as to color when you repaint the office. If the walls have wallpaper on them, check and see if the priest would prefer that the wallpaper be removed, because it's a safe bet that the wallpaper is at least forty years old.

Your priest will probably need a laptop computer. Since clergy often do work at home at night, having the laptop makes work portable. Make sure that your internet or WiFi connection is robust. Cellphones? Sometimes parishes provide a cellphone—your parish will pay for it—or some priests will ask for reimbursement for a portion of the cellphone contract for their existing phone. If you want your priest to be reachable, the cellphone is the most useful way of providing for that.

Make the work space an inviting and comfortable place, but be sure to ask your priest what would make it so. Some of us have particular likes and dislikes, some of us have particular needs, and some of us don't care or worry very much about the space, so ask first!

Hot Issues

In most dioceses, there is an expectation that the prior incumbent makes sure that the new priest knows about particular pastoral concerns, issues that are present in the parish, and other key "priest-to-priest" information that will help the priest begin the work with strength. Sometimes that information comes directly from the prior incumbent and sometimes from the interim. You as the lay leadership may be privy to some of this information, but not all. To the extent that it appears that your new priest has not been informed regarding matters of concern, please do let them know.

Situating Oneself

Your priest may be coming to you from the next town, or the next diocese over, or across the country. It's a new environment. Think about what information might be useful:

- grocery stores,
- trusted professionals like dentists, doctors, lawyers, hair cutters, and plumbers,
- recommended restaurants,
- the library,
- contacts in the police and fire department or the sheriff's office,
- other clergy with whom the parish has a relationship.

There's another aspect of situating oneself, and that is how your parish interacts with other faith communities in your area. In some parts of the country, Episcopal churches are few and far apart; who are the clergypersons from other denominations with whom they may collaborate? In one parish we know, one of the most welcoming groups were the pastors who had long ago come together as a ministerial association. It's always good to have trusted colleagues in the work, whether they are Episcopal priests or not. Someone in your parish might make it a point to let the other pastors in the area know whom you have called and when they are starting, so your new priest can develop a relationship with that group.

If the only Episcopal Church you have ever attended is the one you call home now, it is possible that there are unique traditions or services or events that you may think are widespread throughout the church, but are not. One priest reported that every week in her recent call someone approached her and said, "Aren't you going to do *x*? We always do *x* on the third Sunday after Pentecost." She said that she hadn't heard about that tradition. The person looked at her as if she hadn't been properly trained at seminary. After the third time this happened, the priest realized that she needed to consult with the vestry, the long-time parish secretary, and the altar guild, to craft a master list of the particular traditions in her new parish so she wouldn't be blindsided as she stood in the narthex preparing to begin the service. Make a list. If in doubt whether or not something should go on the list, include it! Information is one of the greatest gifts you can give your priest.

Speaking of information, one of the things your new priest will want to do is to learn your stories. Over time, the priest will build relationships with you, so encourage parishioners to reach out to schedule some time for coffee or tea with your priest to tell their story. Not all in the first week, of course, but over time. Building relationships is the most important first step in ministry . . .

. . . and that means that everyone should have a name tag and wear it! It's a blessing to the priest and the priest's family and it is also a blessing to those parishioners of a certain age for whom a name is just on the tip of the tongue but out of reach. It's also an act of hospitality for newcomers, so getting in the habit of wearing your nametag is helpful in a variety of ways.

Family Matters

If your priest comes with a spouse, understand that there may have been an old tradition that the wife of the priest (and it was always the wife in times past) had the responsibility for pouring the tea or teaching Sunday school or playing the piano. This is a tradition whose time has passed.

You have called the priest. You have not called the spouse. Do not assume particular roles or expect participation in a particular way. One priest's spouse is a nurse whose schedule often meant she was not able to come to church on Sunday mornings. She participated in the life of the parish in a way that worked for her. Another priest's spouse is another priest. That spouse has his own parish and his own responsibilities. Occasionally—and only very occasionally—he comes to the other parish, but his primary responsibility is to his own flock.

Welcome the spouse, to be sure, but let them define how they want to interact. They most likely will not want to be best friends with you because it's a complicated relationship, but you can be warm and welcoming and love them on their own terms.

The same is also true for the children of the priest. They are children, in all their wonderful complexity. They will not be perfect, just as none of us is perfect. They may be shy or they may be outgoing. Welcome them, introduce them to other children their own age, and let things happen naturally.

How can you be helpful? Again, lists of information, like playgrounds, who to talk to in order to get the children registered for school, where the fun restaurants for family dinners might be, stores that are kid-centered, pediatricians, and orthodontists, and such. Have no expectations of them beyond loving them as new parts of your church family. One priest moved several states away. One challenging element of the move was that one of the children had a chronic ailment. When the priest shared that with a couple of members of the discernment committee, it was discovered that a family in the parish had a child with the same ailment. Connections were made and a list of resources specific to that ailment, including the blessed gift of knowing that there was a teaching hospital nearby that had a special clinic for that ailment, made the transition much smoother.

Sometimes the priest's family includes babies or very young children. Out of a desire to be supportive and welcoming, you may want to offer babysitting or minding the children. Some priests' families welcome that, some would prefer not. The priest and spouse know what works best for their children. Respect that.

Lastly, remember that some priests (and their families) are extroverts who are energized by interaction with new people. Some priests are introverts who love people but need a little space and quiet time to function at their best. Whatever you offer in terms of support for your new priest and their family, make it an offer that can be turned down without judgment or repercussions.

The Rectory

All of the same things that were outlined regarding the priest's office apply to the rectory, if you have one. Clean it, fix what needs fixing, update what hasn't been updated in a long time. There may be a tendency on the part of some parishioners who have gifts for interior design to want to execute their vision for the rectory. While the impulse is based in love, excitement, and desire to please, a great gift would be to check in with the priest and the priest's family to see what works for them. Some people want everything painted beige. Some people like bright colors. It's the house that they're going to live in, ideally for some time, so they should be able to share their preferences.

One parish discovered mold and mildew as a result of a leaky toilet. This led to some serious replumbing and replacement of drywall. When it was time to pick out some new fixtures, since two of the toilets had to be replaced, the junior warden sent the priest pictures of the choices so the priest and spouse could select what they preferred. It was such a small thing, but it made the priest feel like they wanted to make the whole family truly welcomed. The junior warden also suggested a brand of paint that was no-VOC (no odor) and asked the priest to let him know what colors they'd like in what rooms. When the priest's family moved in, it already felt a little like their home. Another parish sent floor plans of the rectory to the priest so they could plan how the furnishings would fit in their new environment.

A small but lovely thing; in some parts of the country, there is a tradition of "pounding the rectory." Sounds strange, doesn't it? It involves bringing some things to set up the kitchen and pantry: a pound of butter, a pound of flour, a loaf of bread, a gallon of milk, some breakfast cereal, and so forth. One less thing to worry about after the moving van leaves, and an "outward and visible sign" of grace from the parish and from God.

Some parishes bring casseroles for the freezer. Unless you are certain there are no food allergies, proceed with caution. Particularly if there are children, they may or may not be excited by your award-winning tater tot casserole or that Jello mold. It might be a better gift to give gift cards to some of the local chain restaurants that will be familiar to the youngsters. Ask first what would be helpful.

When Something Goes Sideways

It's not uncommon. The priest says something that inadvertently offends the matriarch of the parish. There's a "Dallas Cowboys" bumper sticker on the priest's car in a rabidly "Chicago Bears" neighborhood. A sermon lands with a resounding clunk. Something slips through the cracks, and someone is angry or hurt.

It happens. Priests are human. The best welcome gift you can offer your new priest is grace, knowing that at some point or other, something will not go well. Do not assume the worst, do not judge, do not turn it into a battle royal, because it usually isn't a battle royal.

What would any of us want when we err? Grace, forgiveness, a chance to make things right. So, too, would priests. We take it as a given that not everything we do will be received as the best thing ever. We do need to know, preferably from the injured party, that we have done something to cause pain or anger. Encourage people to go directly to the priest and talk to them if there is a problem. Do not go to the priest and begin with the phrase, "Some people are saying. . . ." We cannot respond to an amorphous group who are "some people." If someone comes to me and says, "I was offended when you said x. I'm actually very supportive of that group you said bad things about, and I don't think you know what you're talking about," that creates an opportunity for me to say, "I'm sorry. Tell me more about that group. You may be right, I could be wrong, and I'm grateful to learn more." That's the beginning of healing. I can learn why what I said was received badly. I can also learn if my opinion was based on faulty information. I can model, I hope, an open heart and mind. There may also be times when my position is well-founded, and what I need to learn is how to share it in a way that others can hear. Attending to moments of unhappiness when they are relatively small means they might not grow into a long-term wound in the body of Christ.

Remember, too, that context matters. What a priest might be able to make a joke about in Cleveland may be unhelpful in Tallahassee or San Francisco. Let your priest know if that's what is going on.

Let all be based in love and this will be the start of a beautiful friendship.

How Your Diocese Welcomes Your New Priest

Your new priest is not only new to you, they may also be new to your diocese. There are often different ways that dioceses help to integrate new clergy into the life of the diocese. Some have education/networking programs such as Fresh Start. Some have periodic clergy events. Some facilitate continuing education for the clergy.

Whatever activities and events your diocese offers to your new priest, do not begrudge them the time to do these things. Priests vow at their ordination to take part in the larger life of the church, in its councils and in its shared activities. This enriches the priest and it enriches your parish.

Encourage your priest to take advantage of these opportunities, just as you encourage them to take a day off or schedule vacation. Developing networks of colleagues with whom to brainstorm, to share the struggles of the work, to feel a sense of support from those who understand the nature of the work, is critically important to healthy ministry. Your diocese wants that for your priest because your diocese knows that benefits your parish.

XI

---◈---

LAST WORDS

You may think it's over now that your new priest has come. In one sense that's true, of course, but in another, it's simply the start of the next phase of the journey, the one where you think you know where you're going but you are not quite sure. The one where you'll encounter someone who surprises you and changes your angle of view. The one where something happens, because something always happens.

Because God is always doing a new thing. Remember what God says in the book of the prophet Isaiah?

> I am about to do a new thing; now it springs forth, do you not perceive it? I will make a way in the wilderness and rivers in the desert. (Isa. 43:19)

So the journey continues. The difference this time is that you've walked the path through transition and transformation before. You've heard the whisper of the Holy Spirit. You've survived petty moments, sad occasions, disappointments. You've celebrated each milestone and thanked God for them. You've come through the process not merely checking off boxes to get a task done, but trying to discern God's will so you could respond as God desired. You've gotten where God wanted you to go.

So the next new journey might not seem so daunting. You can do this thing, because God is doing it with you. Thanks be to God for you and your faithful service. Bless you and your parish and your priest and whatever the future will hold. We don't know that future, but we do know that God is always doing a new thing, and aren't our hearts strangely warmed by that thought?

And may all God's people, especially those in your parish, say Amen!

APPENDIX A

SAMPLE SURVEYS

Shorter Survey

1. What is your age?

   o Under 12

   o 12–18

   o 19–24

   o 25–34

   o 35–44

   o 45–54

   o 55–64

   o 65 and over

2. What is the approximate travel distance (in miles) from your home to St. Chad's?

   o Under 5 miles

   o 5 to 10 miles

   o 11 to 15 miles

   o 16 to 20 miles

   o Over 20 miles

3. How many years have you been attending St. Chad's?

   o Less than one year

   o 1 to 5 years

   o 6 to 10 years

      ○ 11 to 20 years

      ○ Over 20 years

4. Which service do you usually attend?

      ○ 8:00 a.m. Sunday

      ○ 10:00 a.m. Sunday

      ○ 11:00 a.m. Wednesday Healing Service

5. What first brought you to St. Chad's? (select all that apply)

      ○ Nearest Episcopal church to my home

      ○ Recommended by a friend

      ○ My family attends

      ○ Priest called on me when I moved to the area

      ○ Parishioner called on me when I moved to the area

      ○ Attracted by St. Chad's reputation and historical significance

      ○ Sampled several churches and liked St. Chad's the best

      ○ The Sunday school

      ○ Other, please specify

6. Why have you continued attending St. Chad's? Choose the three (3) most important AND the three (3) least important reasons.

	Most Important	Least Important
Loyalty to the Episcopal Church		
Loyalty to St. Chad's		
I like the people		
A supportive community		
Style of worship appeals to me		
The priest		
The music		

Continued

	Most Important	Least Important
I enjoy participating in one or more of the activities (e.g., choir, Sunday school, outreach, etc.)		
My family has always attended		
I appreciate the opportunities for spiritual growth		
I appreciate the opportunities to serve the church, neighborhood, and local community		
Habit		
Fellowship and chance to share in social activities		
Children/youth activities		

7. If you once attended St. Chad's regularly, but are no longer doing so, please state the reason(s) you are not attending.

_____

_____

_____

_____

_____

8. How important are the various aspects of a worship service to you?

	Less Important	Important	Very Important
A good sermon			
Hymns and anthems			
Traditional hymns			

Continued

	Less Important	Important	Very Important
LEVAS and WLP hymns			
Prayers			
Fellowship/worship with others			
Youth participation			

9. Ritual is the degree of ceremony (high church or low church) we observe in our service. Would you prefer:

- o Same amount of ceremony
- o More ceremony
- o Less ceremony
- o No preference

10. The following is a list of activities, programs, or services offered by our parish. How successful are we?

	Poor	Fair	Good	Have not experienced
Bible study				
Outreach programs–food closet, CARITAS, White Gift, etc.				
Visitation to sick and shut-ins				
Welcoming visitors				
Incorporating new members				
Parish social events				
Youth activities				
Diocesan activities				
Healing service				

Continued

	Poor	Fair	Good	Have not experienced
Building and grounds				
Parish communications				
Community involvement				
Christian education				
Stewardship				
Music				
Sunday school/adult forum				

11. Listed below are some abilities and qualities which a priest might need to perform his/her pastoral responsibilities. Please rate the importance of each of these to you.

	Less Important	Important	More Important
Possession of management and organizational skills			
Involves laity in planning and leading church activities			
Decision making reflects flexibility and respect for laity and other clergy			
Arbiter and mediator of conflicts/disputes			
Participant in diocesan and regional activities			
Supports the world mission of the church			
Develops a strong sense of community among members			

Continued

	Less Important	Important	More Important
Develops a strong sense of stewardship in the congregation			
Brings new members into the fellowship of the church			
Visits the sick and the bereaved			
Visits church members in their homes			
Ability to respond to people at significant points in their lives (dying, death, birth, sickness, success, divorce, etc.)			
Counsels persons facing problems or decisions			
Recognized theologian; knowledgeable in scripture/ theology			
Ability to preach with clarity and to make the gospel relevant in people's lives			
Addresses contemporary issues and ideas			
Tends to be thought-provoking and challenging			
Develops and supports Christian education for youth			
Develops and supports Christian education for adults			
Involved in local community activities and issues			
Involved in critical issues of social justice and concern			

12. Under what type of leadership do you best respond? Specific situations will dictate specific leadership styles. On a scale of 1–5, what style do you prefer?

	Low Preference			Strong Preference	
Authoritative (directs others)	1	2	3	4	5
Coach (trains others)	1	2	3	4	5
Collaborative (works with others)	1	2	3	4	5
Delegator (entrusts others)	1	2	3	4	5
Empowerment (gives power to others)	1	2	3	4	5

13. Have you made a financial pledge to St. Chad's this year?

   o Yes

   o No

14. In this questionnaire, we have asked you to provide specific information on various topics of interest to your discernment committee. Because your responses are critical to our success, we invite you to make any other comments that you feel would be helpful to us in our search for a new priest.

_____

_____

_____

_____

_____

_____

_____

_____

_____

Mid-Length Survey

Dear Fellow Members:

The first phase of the discernment committee process is to gather information about (1) who we are as a church community, which we will use to prepare a description of the parish to attract prospective applicants; and (2) what do we need in our new priest, which we will use to identify the applicant that best matches our needs. The questions below are asked with those objectives in mind. Please have as many people as are willing in your household complete a separate questionnaire.

Note: Your submission can be anonymous, or identified.

Feel free to skip any question!

1. What first attracted you to St. Swithen's? (select all that apply)
   - ☐ Nearest Episcopal Church to my home;
   - ☐ Recommended by a friend;
   - ☐ My family attends;
   - ☐ Priest, parishioner called me when I moved to the area;
   - ☐ Building's charm;
   - ☐ Sermons;
   - ☐ Blue Grass Mass;
   - ☐ Day school;
   - ☐ The number of children;
   - ☐ the music;
   - ☐ Youth fellowship;
   - ☐ An outreach program—name of program: _____;
   - ☐ Other: _____.

2. What is your age?
   - ☐ Under 12;
   - ☐ 12–18;
   - ☐ 19–24;
   - ☐ 25–34;

     □ 45–54;

     □ 55–64;

     □ 65–74;

     □ 75 and over.

3. How many are in your household?____

4. Are you:

     □ Female

     □ Male

5. Are you:

     □ Currently married/have partner;

     □ Widowed;

     □ Divorced;

     □ Single.

6. Are you:

     □ Employed;

     □ Retired;

     □ Looking for work;

     □ Student;

     □ Full-time primary caregiver for another/other (including kids!).

7. Are you so busy (work, family, etc.) that you often miss church but wish you could attend more often:

     □ Yes;

     □ No.

8. What is the approximate travel distance from your home to St. Swithen's?

     □ Under 1/2 mile;

     □ 1/2–1 mile;

     □ 1–2 miles;

     □ 2–5 miles;

     □ Over 5 miles.

9. How many years have you been attending St. Swithen's?

    ☐ less than one year;

    ☐ 1 to 2 years;

    ☐ 2 to 3 years;

    ☐ 3 to 5 years;

    ☐ 5 to 10 years;

    ☐ over 10 years.

10. Which service do you usually attend? (check all that apply)

    ☐ 9:00 a.m. Sunday;

    ☐ 11:00 a.m. Sunday;

    ☐ Bluegrass;

    ☐ Wednesday candlelight service;

    ☐ Coffee and conversation.

11. Ritual is the degree of ceremony (high church or low church) we observe in our service. Would you prefer:

    ☐ Same amount of ceremony;

    ☐ More ceremony;

    ☐ Less ceremony;

    ☐ No preference.

12. If you have a friend that is not active in the church but you think would be interested, what do you think would cause them to become active:

    Comments: _____

13. Is St. Swithen's creating enough opportunities for fellowship for you?

    ☐ Yes;

    ☐ No

    Comment if any:_____

14. Does St. Swithen's offer stewardship options that fit your talents and abilities?

    ☐ Yes;

    ☐ No

    Comment if any:_____

15. Do you believe the St. Swithen's budget matches the parish's values, needs, and sources?

    ☐ Yes;

    ☐ No

    Comment if any:_____

16. Do you believe St. Swithen's properly reaches out to its neighborhood to engage in the community and welcome neighbors to join and participate:

    ☐ Yes;

    ☐ No

    Comment if any:_____

17. In your opinion, is St. Swithen's a spiritually vibrant church:

    ☐ Yes;

    ☐ No

    Comment if any:_____

18. If you once attended St. Swithen's regularly, but are no longer doing so, please share the main reason(s) you are attending less. Please offer feedback to the following by checking all that apply:

This is a big strength of St. Swithen's	Program	This is very important to me	This is less important to me
	Sermons		
	Children's sermon		
	Choir/anthems/solos		
	Open Communion table		
	Traditional hymns		
	LEVAS (newer) hymns		
	Prayers of the people		

Continued

This is a big strength of St. Swithen's	Program	This is very important to me	This is less important to me
	Special prayers		
	Blue Grass Mass		
	Wednesday candlelight service		
	Coffee and conversation		
	Sunday School		
	Church community		
	Youth participation		
	Being family friendly		
	Current church size		
	Church growth		
	Caritas		
	Food closet		
	Visitation to the homebound		
	Pastoral care to the sick, bereaved, people facing difficulties		
	Welcoming visitors		
	Embracing new members		
	Embracing those that society is scorning		
	Parish social events		
	Youth activities		
	Building and grounds		
	Parish communications		
	Supporting the neighborhood		

Continued

This is a big strength of St. Swithen's	Program	This is very important to me	This is less important to me
	Adult faith formation/education		
	Shrine Mont Retreat		
	Annual auction		
	Day school		
	Please add other programs below we have or don't have that you want to address		

19. Please offer feedback about these characteristics in a pastor:

	This is very important to me	This is less important to me
Energetic		
Personable/outgoing		
Deeply spiritual		
Great sermon content and delivery		
Prior experience as a priest		
Prior work experience not as a priest		
Confident–strong personality		
Sense of humor		

Continued

	This is very important to me	This is less important to me
Accessible		
Politically liberal		
Politically moderate		
Politically conservative		
Not openly political		
Possessing strong management and organizational skills		
Involves members in planning and leading church activities		
Decision making reflects flexibility and respect for members and other clergy		
Good arbiter and mediator of conflicts/ disputes		
Participant in diocesan and regional church activities		
Supports the world mission of the church		
Develops a strong sense of community among members		
Develops a strong sense of stewardship in the congregation		
Recognized theologian knowledgeable in scripture/theology		
Addresses contemporary issues and ideas		
Tends to be thought-provoking and challenging		
Gives special attention to Christian education for youth		
Gives special attention to Christian education for adults		

Continued

	This is very important to me	This is less important to me
Involved in critical issues of social justice and concern		
Please add below additional characteristics of importance		

20. Would you like to see St. Swithen's using technology more in the following:

	No	Yes: If yes, please comment on what you would like to see done.
Services		
Music		
Coffee and conversation		
Our website		
Our e-mails		

Comment:_____

21. Would you like to meet with someone on the discernment committee?

     ☐ Yes: My name and contact info is: _____

     [*WARNING: This is an optional question and offers the possibility for further dialogue, but weakens the sense of confidentiality.*]

22. Please offer any suggestions for the discernment committee (such as names of possible candidates; questions to ask; priorities to have; ways to communicate with the parish; etc.):

     Thank you for your input!

The Priest Discernment Committee: Survey Roll-Up Sample

St. F Parish Survey Results (N=185)

Demographic Information:

Age:

    51–65 (40%)

    Over 65 (30%)

    36–50 (22%)

    19–24 (3%)

    12–18 (3%)

Gender:

    Female (61%)

    Male (38%)

    Prefer not to answer (1%)

Marital status:

    Married (74%)

    Single (9%)

    Divorced (7%)

    Widowed (6%)

    Prefer not to answer (2%)

    Living with partner (1%)

Children in household:

    No children (55%)

    Middle/high school (27%)

    Elementary school (16%)

    Graduated college living at home (9%)

    Children beyond age 25 living at home (5%)

    Preschool (3%)

How long attended services at St. F?

> Over ten years (68%)
> 6 to 10 years (21%)
> 1 to 5 years (10%)
> Less than 1 year (1%)

Survey Questions—St. F Today

What activities are important to you? (10 choices):

> Top Three
> Worship (86%)
> Sermon (85%)
> Fellowship (84%)

"The priest's most visible role is in the pulpit. This is where he/she makes the strongest impression.

Being able to deliver a strong, meaningful, and memorable sermon is critical. . . ."

Current Parish Life—What are our strengths and weaknesses?
(36 choices)

Particular Strength	Particular Weakness
Choir (80%)	Youth Activities Overall (22%)
Grounds (72%)	Youth Service Opportunities (25%)
Country Fair (64%)	Youth Social Activities (25%)

"I think we haven't given our youth enough time just to be kids and hang with unscheduled activities. . . . It used to be more about having friends at church and knowing that you are always welcome. Our church youth group was a fun group that included several nonmembers and we all had fond memories. I don't think our youth (now) have that bonding time."

"We need more emphasis on youth and adult mission trips. We need to instill the ideals of service and fellowship among our youth and between youth and adults. THIS IS CRITICALLY IMPORTANT."

"Youth activities, programs, etc. were very weak and/or unappealing to my children . . . especially when compared to those offered by friends' churches."

ABILITIES OF A NEW PRIEST: How much attention should the priest devote to the following areas? (10 choices)

Significant/Highest Attention	Lowest/Modest Amount of Attention
Parish Spiritual Life (86%)	Parish Administration (31%)
Pastoral Care (77%)	Ecumenical/Community (27%)
Youth (76%)	Music (23%)

"I was hoping (my child) would have more opportunities to speak with Ben— who was the first youth leader he could relate to. I hope we can find some-one . . . that can really relate to the young adult and teens—because (my child) had doubts and questioned God and religion too."

What are the areas which are most important for leadership by the new priest? (10 choices)

Most Important	Least Important
Parish Spiritual Life (75%)	Ecumenical/Community (18%)
Pastoral Care (71%)	Administration (19%)
Youth Activities (59%)	Stewardship (21%)

"The priest should attend to the theological needs of the congregation and the vestry should attend to the secular needs."

I prefer a priest who: (19 choices)

Most Important (scale)

Is Outgoing (77%)

Regards the Bible as an Interpretation of God's Dealing with Humanity (68%)

Has a Conversational/Informal Delivery (68%)

"We need an outgoing, charismatic, energetic, and gregarious priest who can inspire folks to be part of a vibrant parish. Please, no administrators or individuals with an agenda."

"The real question is whether or not our priest should view the Bible as having timeless authority—or whether that authority should be reinterpretable and changed based on people's views in each age. . . . God is timeless and does not change."

If deemed legal, the priest should perform same-sex marriage:[1]

Agree/Strongly Agree (56%) Disagree/Strongly Disagree (28%)

The priest should be permitted to perform blessings of same-sex unions for members:

Agree/Strongly Agree (70%) Disagree/Strongly Disagree (16%)

"I don't get particularly worked up about the issue of same sex marriage. What WOULD get me worked up is if the new priest spent a great deal of time on issues like that and not on further development of the parish."

"My views on same sex marriage have changed from disapproval to approval over the past six years. I want same sex couples to have the same opportunity to have a committed relationship that is blessed by and respected by the community."

"We should make our church open and welcoming to the gay community. We routinely forgive the sins of the Ten Commandments. Leviticus is pretty explicit in declaring homosexuality a sin. Just as we do NOT act to encourage or accept sin, we should not encourage the sin of homosexuality by holding a ceremony to celebrate it."

ST. F of the Future

Social justice . . . which response captures your view?

I think St. F strikes the right balance. (61%)

I would support a social action ministry. (26%)

The Episcopal church is too progressive/should return to traditional roots. (13%)

---

1. This survey was done several years ago before marriage of same-gender persons was legal in our state, and attitudes have changed dramatically in our diocese, as they have throughout the nation. It is interesting to note, though, how varied the responses quoted were. If this survey was presented in the same parish today, it would most likely yield markedly different results.

"I believe we are called to minister in the world, but if we enter into active engagement with the larger church on divisive social issues, I believe it will split our balanced church which now functions in a community of shared, overarching Christian spirit despite very divergent political and social opinions among its (not shy) membership."

"I would support a social action ministry but only if it is not a divisive issue in the congregation."

"The Episcopal Church is too progressive and is forcing its viewpoint on local churches. . . . St. F thus far has done a good job of trying to strike the right balance."

"Regarding social justice—we may strike the right balance today, but need to be prepared to lead and anticipate a more active position. I bet the people in [A city which experienced racial unrest] thought they had the right balance."

Given sufficient resources . . . what would you like to see? (Six choices)

Highest Ranking (list)

> Social and intellectual programs for retirees (53%)
>
> Teen center (35%)
>
> Music or fine arts education program (35%)

"Not just retirees for intellectual programs. Why not for all ages?"

Narrative Question: What excites you most about the future of St. F? (no choices offered)

Most frequent response: Growth in membership (27%)

"Knowledge that great resources in talent among our parishioners gives us potential to accomplish almost anything we might attempt."

Narrative Question: If St. F disappeared . . . what would you miss most? (no choices offered)

Most frequent response: Fellowship/Community (84%)

"I hope St. F continues to be a place where families of various political views (are) drawn together in their mutual belief in a loving God and where they can practice that love with each other."

Some Guidelines for the Conduct of Focus Groups

Focus groups allow researchers to study the opinions, interests, needs, and aspirations of people who are members of a given group (a congregation, for example) in a group conversation, a more natural setting than a one-on-one interview. Properly administered, the participants are freer to share and in that way the researcher can learn the stories, customs, and even the vernacular of a group. Focus groups are "observer dependent," so that their validity is a function of the carefulness and independence of the researcher.

I. Focus group—definition

    a. a small group, six to ten people, led through a discussion that lasts no more than ninety minutes by a researcher,

    b. structured around predetermined open-ended questions designed to stimulate discussion among the members,

    c. who are relatively homogeneous (grouped by gender, age, interests, or affiliations) to encourage openness.

II. Focus groups are not:

    a. debates,

    b. problem-solving discussions, or

    c. group therapy.

III. The questions

    a. Short, unambiguous, open-ended (cannot be answered by "yes" or "no.")

    b. Can be "fill in the blank" types.

    c. Cannot be threatening or appear to "poke a stick in a hornet's nest."

IV. Three types:

    a. Engagement—make the participants feel welcome and at ease.

    b. Elaboration—dig into the meat of the discussion.

    c. Exit—check to see what was missed in the conversation.

V. Preparation of the participants

    a. Focus groups may be recruited in a number of ways:

        i. Random selection—a random number applied to a large group (members of the congregation or, in a large congregation, members of the same activity group).

        ii. All members of the same group—for example, members of the volunteer choir, the bridge club, the men's breakfast.

        iii. Nomination—key members nominate people they think would be helpful and not burdened with an agenda.

        iv. Self-selection—this approach may make good sense diplomatically, but the results are probably to be discounted.

    b. Issue a formal invitation with a follow-up reminder.

    c. Over-invite by 20 percent.

    d. Offer an incentive (e.g., a meal, a desert, gift certificates, etc.—though most people are flattered to be included).

    e. Also offer childcare or transportation as appropriate.

    f. Arrange comfortable chairs in a circle for the meeting.

VI. Conducting the focus group

    a. Ideally, there should be a moderator and an assistant. The moderator asks the questions and the assistant takes notes and, if possible, manages the voice recorder.

    b. The best moderators are able to listen carefully, keep their own opinions out of the conversation, and engage all members of the group in the conversation.

       i. Careful listening means not formulating the next question while someone is answering the last, but listening with all the senses, observing body language, etc.

      ii. Follow-up questions require that the moderator be flexible, shaping the follow-up questions to elicit more depth of understanding, especially when the issue is important or unclear.

c. The assistant moderator is able to take notes, not only of salient points, but also of what is not spoken (body language, facial expression, etc.).

d. The moderator has the responsibility to elicit as much information as possible in the time allotted. To that end, the moderator must be aware of:

       i. Self-appointed experts: "Thank you. What do other people think?"

      ii. The dominator: "Let's have some other comments."

     iii. The rambler: Stop eye contact; look at your watch; jump in at their inhale.

     iv. The shy participant: Make eye contact; call on them; smile at them.

      v. The participant who talks very quietly: Ask them to repeat their response more loudly.

     vi. "Groupthink": The tendency for more influential members of the group to affect others.

e. The moderator must remain neutral—no nodding of the head, no raised eyebrows, no affirmation of agreeable ideas.

VII. Analyzing the data

a. Immediately after the session, the moderator and assistant must compare notes and record their conclusions. If the group is being recorded, this should also be recorded.

b. In reviewing the conversation, it is helpful to create a spreadsheet looking for commonalities in the areas of interest and the reaction to them.

        i. areas of interest can be grouped into categories,

       ii. participants given numbers, and

     iii. comments recorded in brief.

   c. This data can then be synthesized for presentation.

Example:

Welcome:

"Thanks for agreeing to be part of this focus group. I am the moderator and Jane is the assistant moderator. Our jobs are as follows: _____.

The purpose of this focus group is to explore with you your experience of St. Martin's at present, your hopes and dreams for St. Martin's, and whatever concerns you may have about the future.

We want you to do all the talking. This is not a test; there are no right or wrong answers; and what is said in this room will stay in this room. After the session, we will analyze what has been said for further use by the (vestry, discernment committee, etc.)."

Begin with an easy icebreaker:

   "If money were no issue, where in the world would you like to visit most?"
   "What is the strangest food you have ever eaten?"

Follow with an easy first question on point:

   "My favorite memory of St. Martin's is. . . ."
   "I first came to St. Martin's because . . ."
   "The time that I was the happiest at St. Martin's was when . . ."
   "St. Martin's feels most like the church I want my grandchildren to love when . . ."

Be prepared to follow up with questions that dig deeper:

"Could you say more about that?"
"Can you give us an example?"

And at the end:

"Thank you for coming. Your comments have been most helpful and will be important in the work of the committee."

Adapted from the Office of Assessment, Duke University

APPRECIATIVE INQUIRY-STYLE CONGREGATIONAL MEETING

Congregational Meeting Agenda[1]

Opening Prayer and Welcome (5 min)

Introductions:

Why we are here; agenda preview; search process; what's next (10 min)

Explanation of Meeting Process: Appreciative Inquiry introduction; small group formation (10 min)

Small Group Input

Every voice is heard (90 minutes in all)

Set up: tables of 6 participants, 1 facilitator, sticky notes, chart paper

QUESTION 1

Reflect on your time in our congregation. Locate a moment that was a high point, when you felt our church was doing God's work/fulfilling its mission.

Task 1 (20 min)

- Talk about your experience: In pairs, interview each other using Question 1.
- Share your responses with the table group, documenting your responses on sticky notes.
- In your table group, identify the themes. On sticky notes, write what was happening during the high point, and place on the chart paper.

---

1. Adapted from the process used by the Diocese of North Carolina.

Whole group:

Debrief Question 1 themes with whole group (5 min)

QUESTION 2

Name the three things you value most about our congregation.

Task 2 (20 min)

- Talk about your experience: In pairs, interview each other using Question 2.
- Share your responses with the table group, documenting your responses on sticky notes.
- In your table group, identify the themes. On sticky notes, write the three things you value most, and place on the chart paper.

Whole group:

Debrief Question 2 themes with whole group. (5 min)

QUESTION 3

What do you hope our congregation's three most important accomplishments over the next three to five years will be? What is God calling us to be? Why does God want us here, now?

Task 3 (20 min)

- Talk about your experience: In pairs, interview each other using Question 3.
- Share your responses with the table group, documenting your responses on sticky notes.
- In your table group, identify the themes. On sticky notes, write the three things you hope the congregation will accomplish in the next three to five years, and place on the chart paper.

Whole group:

Debrief Question 3 themes with whole group. (5 min)

WHOLE GROUP DEBRIEF

What do you think about as you see this work? (10 min)

CLOSING PRAYER

COMMUNITY MINISTRY PORTFOLIO WORKSHEET

Sample Template

Please understand that this format is not decided by your diocese, but by the Episcopal Church.

Instructions about formatting and suggestions on content in red.

SECTION I: BASIC INFORMATION

Name of worshipping community:

Diocese: Virginia

Current Status: Receiving names

We recommend only posting the portfolio when the church is receiving names. Other options are: beginning search, seeking interim, interim in place, developing self-study, developing profile, profile complete, no longer receiving names, reopened, and search complete.

Order of ministry required:

- ☐ Bishop
- ☐ Deacon
- ☐ Lay
- ☐ Lay or Ordained
- ☐ Priest

Position title (e.g., priest, vicar, priest-in-charge):

Possible options:

Priest/vicar/priest-in charge

Priest/vicar/priest-in-charge (part-time)

Assistant/associate/curate

Assistant/associate/curate (part-time)

Interim

OTM doesn't allow you to pick one, e.g., "vicar" or "associate," as they appear on each line above is how they appear in the dropdown menu.

Receiving Names until:

Format: "January 19, 2015"

Weekly Average Sunday Attendance (ASA):

Numbers only, no commas.

Number of Weekend Worship Services:

Numbers only, no commas.

Number of Weekday Worship Services:

Numbers only, no commas.

Number of Other per Month Worship Services:

Numbers only, no commas.

Institution Phone:

Institution E-mail:

Use the same e-mail you would for contact below.

Institution Address:

Contact Name:

In the case of a priest search, use the search chair or cochairs. In the case of an associate/assistant search, use the priest or search chair, if applicable.

Contact E-mail:

We strongly recommend that the discernment committee set up a separate e-mail address that only the discernment committee members or chair(s) can see. E-mail accounts shared by spouses may not be used.

Contact Phone 1:

Contact Phone 2:

Contact Address:

For candidates who will be mailing materials, we recommend using the chair's home address to protect the confidentiality of the candidates. You may also indicate that the discernment committee only wishes to receive electronic submissions.

SECTION II: COMPENSATION HOUSING & BENEFITS

Current Annual Compensation (Includes the following [check all that apply]):

What you're currently paying is irrelevant. Don't put anything here. Focus on what you have available to pay your next priest (see "Compensation Available for New Position" below.) The vestry will give you that number.

Cash Stipend ☐

Checking this box indicates that your worshipping community will provide housing in the form of a cash stipend as compared to a specific place to live, such as a rectory.

Cash Stipend Detail:

Numbers only, no commas.

Housing / Rectory Detail (annually):

Numbers only, no commas.

Utilities: ☐

Checking this box indicates that your worshipping community will pay housing utilities. (Note: Churches providing a cash stipend will typically factor that amount into the stipend. Paying utilities is more common for churches provid-ing rectory.)

Utilities Detail:

Numbers only, no commas.

SECA reimbursement: ☐

Checking this box indicates that you will pay some portion of the SECA reimbursement.

SECA reimbursement options (Choose One):

☐ N/A

☐ Full

☐ Half

☐ Other

SECA reimbursement details:

Compensation Available for New Position:

Numbers only, no commas.

Negotiable (Choose One):

☐ N/A

☐ Yes

☐ No

Additional Compensation Note:

Limit 100 characters including spaces. Often used to provide more details about compensation not available from selection above.

Housing Available for persons:

Numbers only. If you'll be paying a housing allowance, leave blank. This is intended to indicate the size of your rectory, if applicable.

Pension Plan: We're in compliance with CPF requirements.

Healthcare Options (Choose One):

- □ N/A
- □ Full family
- □ Clergy+1
- □ Clergy only
- □ Negotiable

Dental (Choose One):

- □ N/A
- □ Yes
- □ No

Housing Equity Allowance in budget (Choose One):

- □ None
- □ Yes
- □ No
- □ Negotiable

Housing equity is for churches who will provide a rectory/housing. Housing equity is money paid to the priest to make up for the equity they lose out on by not owning his/her own home.

Annual Equity Amount:
Numbers only, no commas.

Vacation Weeks (Choose One):

- □ 4
- □ One month, including 5 Sundays (Standard)
- □ Other

Vacation Weeks Details:

Numbers only, no commas.

Continuing Education Weeks (2 weeks (Standard) or Other):

- ☐ 2 (standard)
- ☐ Other

Continuing Education Weeks Details:

Numbers only, no commas. Use if you selected "other."

Continuing Education Funding in budget (Choose One):

- ☐ up to / including $500/year
- ☐ $501–$1000 / year
- ☐ $1001–$2000 / year
- ☐ over $2000 / year

Sabbatical Provision (Choose One):

- ☐ N/A
- ☐ Yes
- ☐ No

Travel/Auto Account (Choose One):

- ☐ N/A
- ☐ Yes
- ☐ No

Other Professional Account (Choose One):

- ☐ N/A
- ☐ Yes
- ☐ No

Comments:

100 character limit, including punctuation and spaces. Often used to give information, details that couldn't be expressed in the template above.

SECTION III: WORK HISTORY & SKILLS

Names of previous incumbents. That is, if the position is for priest, list previous priests and interim priests in chronological order. You can leave out associate/assistant priests. You may list up to three.

Name:

Position Title:

Date Begun (MM/YYYY):

Date Ended (MM/YYYY):

Name:

Position Title:

Date Begun (MM/YYYY):

Date Ended (MM/YYYY):

Name:

Position Title:

Date Begun (MM/YYYY):

Date Ended (MM/YYYY):

Church School:

Name of school (e.g., Sunday school, Sunday Christian formation). Include youth groups and young adult ministry as Teen/Young Adults School (we apologize on OTM's behalf that those two are counted together, we realize they're very different ministries).

Number of Teachers/Leaders for Children School:

Numbers only, no commas.

Number of Students for Children School:

Numbers only, no commas.

Number of Teachers/Leaders for Teen/Young Adults School:

Numbers only, no commas.

Number of Students for Teen/Young Adults School:

Numbers only, no commas.

Number of Teachers/Leaders for Adults School:

Numbers only, no commas.

Number of Students for Adults School:

Numbers only, no commas.

Day School:

- ☐ Pre-K
- ☐ Kindergarten
- ☐ K-6
- ☐ K-12
- ☐ Other

Number of Students for Day School:

Numbers only, no commas.

Number of Teachers for Day School:

Numbers only, no commas.

Number of Total Staff for Day School:

Numbers only, no commas.

Notes:

500 character limit, including punctuation and spaces. This space can be used to give more detail, to breakdown the numbers above, or to write (briefly) about a ministry you're especially proud of, for example, "Christ Church's preschool is one of the best preschools in the county" or "We are proud to say we have one of the largest twenties and thirties groups in the diocese."

SECTION IV: NARRATIVE

In our baptism we promise to proclaim by word and example the Good News of God in Christ, seeking and serving Christ in all persons. You are invited here to reflect on your ministry by responding to all of the following questions (in 1,200 characters each, including spaces and punctuation). You may answer in more than one language, if appropriate.

As you respond to the following questions, rather than generalize, we recommend that you tell a short, illustrative story and briefly explain what that says about who you are as a church.

Describe a moment in your worshipping community's recent ministry which you recognize as one of success and fulfillment.

1,200 character limit, including punctuation and spaces.

Describe your liturgical style and practice. If your community provides more than one type of worship service, please describe all:

1,200 character limit, including punctuation and spaces.

How do you practice incorporating others in ministry?

1,200 character limit, including punctuation and spaces.

Note: this is not necessarily about incorporating folks in worship, though it may include that. Take a broader view, which might include ministries like outreach volunteers, Sunday school teachers, ushers, vestry service, etc.

As a worshipping community, how do you care for your spiritual, emotional, and physical well-being?

1,200 character limit, including punctuation and spaces.

Describe your worshipping community's involvement in either the wider church or geographical region.

1,200 character limit, including punctuation and spaces.

How do you engage in pastoral care for those beyond your worshipping community?

1,200 character limit, including punctuation and spaces.

Tell about a ministry that your worshipping community has initiated in the past five years. Who can be contacted about this?

1,200 character limit, including punctuation and spaces.

How are your preparing yourselves for the church of the future?

1,200 character limit, including punctuation and spaces.

What is your practice of stewardship and how does it shape the life of your worshipping community?

1,200 character limit, including punctuation and spaces.

What is your worshipping community's experience of conflict? How have you addressed it?

1,200 character limit, including punctuation and spaces.

What is your experience leading change in the church? When has it gone well? When has it gone poorly? What did you learn?

1,200 character limit, including punctuation and spaces.

Please provide words describing the gifts and skills essential to the future leaders of your worshipping community.

Use up to four short phrases here, e.g., inspired preaching, visionary leader, teacher, community organizer, etc.

SECTION V: CONNECTIONS

Your worshipping community's website:

You may provide the media links to your worshipping community:
They may be audio, video, YouTube, etc. Include the exact web addresses for linked media.

You may provide links here to other sites where you might be found:
Include the exact web addresses.

Languages significantly represented in your worshipping community:

Please indicate the total percentage of your Average Sunday Attendance that worships in a language other than English. __%

Numbers and decimal points only, no commas.

Approximate number of people:

Provide worship or classes in the following languages:

Notes (100 Words):

SECTION VI: REFERENCES

Bishop Name: The Rt. Rev. XXXXXX

Bishop Contact Information:

Diocesan Transition Ministry Officer Name:

Diocesan Transition Ministry Officer Contact Information:

Current Warden/Board Chair Name:

Current Warden/Board Chair Contact Information:

In most cases it wouldn't be appropriate for a candidate to contact the senior warden directly, so just include name without contact information.

Previous Warden/Board Chair Name:

Previous Warden/Board Chair Contact Information:

In most cases it wouldn't be appropriate for a candidate to contact the previous senior warden directly, so just include name without contact information.

Search Chair Name:

Search Chair Ministry:

(e.g., chair or cochair)

Search Chair Contact Information:

Phone number and e-mail address, preferably an e-mail address only the discernment committee chair or discernment committee have access to. Example: priestsearch.stswythens@gmail.com

Parish/Institution Leader Name:

Parish/Institution Leader Ministry:

Parish/Institution Leader Contact Information:

Local Community Leader Name:

This is a leader in your town or city (e.g. mayor, city council member, local food pantry coordinator, etc.) who is familiar with your ministry.

Local Community Leader Relationship:

Local Community Leader Contact Information:

Guidance for Vestries to Understand the Compensation Section (Section II) of the CMP

Attached is an excerpt from the community ministry portfolio (CMP). The portfolio is a template created by the Episcopal Church's Office of Transition Ministry (OTM) that appears in a database which clergy with access can search.[1] The template covers the church's demographics, compensation, history, challenges, and vision for the future.

The portfolio is drafted in its entirety by the discernment committee, save Section II (Compensation, Housing & Benefits), which is drafted by the vestry. The discernment committee will engage in work of self-study and present a final candidate to the vestry. The vestry approves the budget of the discernment committee, issues a call to the discernment committee's nominee (God willing), and negotiates the compensation package.

Section II of the community ministry portfolio sets out expectations for compensation and benefits for potential candidates while allowing room for negotiation.

Definition of Terms

Diocesan Minimum Compensation Guidelines and More Info

- Check your diocesan website or talk to your diocesan staff to see if there are compensation guidelines that apply as you calculate what compensation will look like for the position.

- In some dioceses, those guidelines are tied to number of years of ordained experience. In others, the size of the parish is taken into consideration. In yet others, it's a mixture. Parishes should note that when the guidelines stipulate minimums, these are minimums for the work to be considered full-time, and generally don't represent a competitive salary. Contact your transition ministry officer for information on comparable compensation figures.

---

1. *www.otmportfolio.org*. Note that access to this database is limited to clergy and transition ministers.

"**Compensation**" includes the cash stipend, housing, SECA (and in case of a rectory, utilities and housing equity as well).

- **Cash stipend:** All of the priest's salary that is not designated for housing or SECA.
- **Housing:** For tax purposes, priests designate a certain portion of their compensation as housing. However, how this is broken up is up to the priest, so we recommend that vestries include the total available for cash, housing, and SECA.
- **SECA:** The church contributes 7.65% of priest's total compensation, which is half of the 15.3% priests are expected to pay. SECA stands for the "Self-Employed Contributions Act Tax." In the eyes of the IRS, clergy are self-employed.
- Additional compensation **if the priest will be living in the rectory**:
- **Utilities:** Churches may pay the cost of the utilities on the rectory.
- **Housing Equity Allowance:** Housing equity is money paid to the priest to make up for the equity they lose out on by not owning his/her own home. This is not required but may be requested as part of the negotiation between the priest and the vestry.

"**Benefits**" includes pension, healthcare, dental, continuing education, vacation, and sabbatical.

- **Pension:** The Church Pension Group requires an 18% contribution to every priest's pension (Pension=Total Annual Compensation X .18).
- **Healthcare:** The diocese offers several competitive healthcare plan options for single, single+spouse, single+child, and full family. Costs for these plans usually can be found in a link within your diocese's compensation guidelines.
- **Dental:** Costs are also usually listed in compensation guidelines.
- **Continuing Education:** $500 has been typical for small churches, but will only cover registration for a conference, not travel or other expenses. Churches, especially larger ones, should consider making room in the budget for their priest to attend conferences for professional development.

- **Vacation:** The standard is four weeks' vacation, including five Sundays. We believe this is essential for health of the priest and the priest's family. The five Sunday provision allows the priest to take one or more continuous weeks off.
- **Sabbatical:** Typically three months' paid leave after five to seven years of service. It is intended to rejuvenate the priest and, by extension, the life of the parish.

Professional/Travel Accounts:

- **Professional Account:** this might include hospitality costs if the priest is taking a parishioner to lunch, for example, or hosting a meeting of the local clergy association. It might also include books for professional development or participation in a local nonprofit meeting that might have benefits for the parish.
- **Travel Account:** this might include reimbursable mileage at current IRS rates for professional use of the priest's personal vehicle—one round trip between home and church per day is excepted as normal commutation—or it might include the leasing of a vehicle for the priest, if it makes more sense economically for the parish. If you choose to cap the amount, remember how quickly such funds can be depleted by hospital visits to parishioners, particularly if the hospital(s) is/are distant from the community, and if the parish has many elderly members. Keep in mind the cost of tolls if the normal travel routes require traveling on toll roads.
- **Discretionary Fund:** The discretionary fund isn't considered compensation or benefits, as clergy must use it for specifically "pious and charitable uses" as detailed in the canons of the Episcopal Church. Thus, the funds cannot be used for the personal benefit of the clergy but are to be used to assist those in need. Discretionary funds are ubiquitous across the Church so they don't need to be mentioned in the CMP.

Participation in the Councils of the Church:

- Priests are expected to participate in diocesan activities such as diocesan convention, clergy conferences, and other diocesan-required programs.

These are neither benefits to be delineated in the CMP nor are they vacation or continuing education; they are canonically designated requirements. Thus, budgetary consideration must be made for them, but they are not considered part of the compensation package. Different parishes handle the costs of activities such as diocesan convention or clergy conferences in their budgets differently. We mention this simply to remind the vestry to reserve funds for these activities.